PRAISE FOR

"THE SPIRAL PATHWAY OF GRIEF"

"I just completed reading "*The Spiral Pathway of Grief*" for the second time. I wish that book had been published so much earlier. The author has a Master's in Social Work and many years of experience as a grief counselor. I believe that every single adult human being has experienced a major loss at some point in their lives. It may be the loss of a loved one, a job, an important asset or anything held dear. A loss causes humans much grief that we do not know how to handle. This book will prove invaluable to everyone."

   -Gail Baiman, author, hypnotherapist, Prosperity Teacher and Master Firewalk Instructor.

"My life experience has shown me that life is a series of losses because any time there's change there's loss. This book reinforces my belief that we can learn and heal. It has been and will continue to be a guide for me in my journey."
-Rebecca Stover, Crone

"Grace writes from the Heart and is right from the heart. If ever there's a time when we need an updated guide to navigate loss and grief, it would be now. Well done, Grace, very well done."
-Ken Donaldson. L.M.F.T., author of *Marry Yourself First*
https://kendonaldson.com/

"'Amazing Grace,' you are not only an angel you are a profound and prolific counselor/consultant. The authenticity of your book is so helpful ...this book should help many to transform and speak openly to grief. You make ownership of our grief personal and relievable. Addressing outdated approaches shines a light on self-inflicted wounds and imposed societal restrictions. You have identified a path to releasing grief and you provide resources for transformation. You have provided facts opposed to myths and misconceptions. Another book to utilize for reference and guidance. Thanks for inspiring us to know we can grieve differently and that we can receive help. So grateful for your commitment to serve and share. Very impressive book."
-Rosa Cambridge, MMIN, RN, BSN, CM; President, Tampa FL Chapter of National Black Nurses Association; Past President, Metropolitan Tampa, FL, Section, National Council of Negro Women

---

"What a relief to read an honest integration of grief. Our humanness is woven together with the threads of loss and change. Grace invites us to loosen the binds of old patterns of processing grief."
-Rev. Dr. Martha Creek, New Thought/Ancient Wisdom Teacher, www.marthacreek.com

---

"Ms. Terry is a warm and compassionate grief mentor whose sensitive guidance through the grieving process is based on both years of professional education and experience and deep wisdom gained through personal experience on her own grief journey. Highly recommended - I wish this book had been available when I was first traveling on my own grief path."
-Anne Sulli, MA, Reiki Master, Interfaith Minister

"Grief can be a devastating or a positively transformative experience in our lives, and finally we have a clear, practical, and profound guide to this universal experience. In *The Spiral Pathway of Grief*, Grace Terry shares her decades of experience with grief counseling to compassionately liberate us from pervasive misunderstandings and well-meaning falsehoods about the grief process. We all grieve at some point, and this book is an outstanding resource of wisdom to bring light to our world."
-Will Tuttle Ph.D., author of the best-selling book, *The World Peace Diet*, is a recipient of the *Courage of Conscience Award*, the co-founder of Circle of Compassion, and an acclaimed pianist and composer. www.willtuttle.com

As a person who is currently grieving this book brought much insight. I particularly hope readers pay attention to myth #12. This book was like a homecoming of healing wrapped in a blanket.
-Linda Burhans, author, caregiver advocate, talk show host

THE SPIRAL PATHWAY OF GRIEF

A TRAVELER'S GUIDEBOOK

GRACE TERRY, MSW

CONTENTS

Ten Simple Strategies for
A Happier You

Changing the World From the Inside Out

GRACE TERRY, MSW

Other books by Grace Terry, MSW: *Ten Simple Strategies for a Happier You: Changing the World from the Inside Out*

DEDICATION

This book is dedicated to all the angels
who have guided and comforted me
on my journey through grief.
Some are flesh and blood human angels.
Some are celestial.
Some are family and friends.
Some were strangers who went
out of their way to be kind.
Some are furry and four-legged.
Some are musicians, poets, artists, authors –
both living and immortal.

All helped to make me the person I am today:
relatively sane, reasonably functional,
still learning as I plod the spiral pathway,
peaceful most of the time,
and daily grateful.

DISCLAIMER

This publication is designed to provide competent and reliable information regarding the subject matter covered. It is sold with the understanding that the author/publisher is not engaged in rendering financial, legal, psychotherapeutic, medical or other professional advice through this publication. If the reader requires expert assistance to address individual needs, the services of a competent professional should be sought.

The ideas/strategies/suggestions recorded here were collected by the author over a lifetime of study, exploration, and seeking. Every word of this text is true in the author's personal experience. Your mileage may vary. Take what works for you and leave the rest.

Every effort has been made to make this volume as accurate as possible. However, there could be mistakes or errors, both typographical and in content. Therefore this text should be used only as a general guide and not as the ultimate source of information or direction. The Ultimate Source of information and direction resides within each reader.

In the event the reader uses any of the information and/or suggestions in this book, the author/publisher assumes no responsibility or liability for your actions.

ABOUT THE AUTHOR

Grace Terry is a wise woman in the sacred tradition of the wounded healer. In transcending her own challenges with multiple traumatic losses, childhood abuse and neglect, clinical depression and anxiety, chronic pain and disordered eating, she gained skills, knowledge and wisdom which she generously passes forward to others today.

With expertise in many areas of holistic wellness, her favorite role is that of grief educator/mentor/coach/companion. She is also a sacred storyteller, ordained interfaith minister, retreat and workshop leader, and an inspirational/motivational speaker. With compassion, eloquence, humor and finely attuned intuition, she is a transformative channel for healing and peace.

Grace is available for individual, family or small group consultation, for leading workshops and retreats, and for keynote speaking. At the time of this writing she is facilitating grief resolution groups and webinars virtually on a regular basis.

To schedule a personal consultation or to discuss sponsoring an event with Grace, you can schedule time with her through her website www.angelsabide.com. You can also send her an email message through the website. The first half-hour "get acquainted" session is free. Beyond that, Grace's fees are moderate and flexible. Her greatest desire is to pass forward the kindness that has been generously shown to her.

ACKNOWLEDGEMENTS

This book has been in the making since 1984, the year I experienced three traumatic losses. The first was sudden, unexpected termination of employment. Before I found a new position there was a sudden, unexpected divorce and relocation. The third was the sudden, unexpected death of my beautiful, vibrant fifty-six year old mother in an automobile accident.

When my mother died, friends, family, and strangers showed me great kindness. The love and support was absolutely palpable and brought me back from the only agnostic period of my life, the few months between my divorce and my mother's death.

Since then, there have been additional losses - my father's sudden death two years after my mother's, a second divorce a year after that, devastating betrayals, forced estrangement, financial reverses, and others. Miraculously, many kind and caring people appeared over the years to guide and comfort me on the spiral pathway of grief.

I once knew a man who said, "Desperation is my best friend." I believe my angels and grief companions appeared in my life because I desperately sought their guidance and was willing to accept it. It was a matter of survival. I knew I had to have help or I wouldn't make it.

On the dedication page of this book, I acknowledge all who have loved me through life's most challenging twists, turns, and transitions. Without the on-going compassion and kindness of countless angels along the way, I could not have written a book worth publishing.

I must also acknowledge all those who allowed me the privilege of being a companion on their grief journeys. I have learned so much from you and I appreciate you more than I can ever say.

Three special people contributed their gifts to the creation of this book manuscript, resulting in a final publication that is far superior to anything I might have created on my own:

- Jim Auxier, my incredible husband, life partner, in-house technical support person, and editorial assistant who faithfully and lovingly supports my efforts to make a positive difference with my life;
- Cathy Williams Crawford, my sister, who took time from her very demanding legal services practice to provide skillful editorial assistance and content consultation;
- Anne Sulli, my dear friend and a member of my family of choice, an accomplished writer herself, who provided encouragement and emotional support as well as excellent proofreading, editing and content consultation.

Additionally, Bogdan Stancu (contact: bogdan@internetmarket-inglight.com) adapted my book cover design from a watercolor painted especially for me by intuitive artist Madeleine Tuttle (www.willtuttle.com).

Michael Lacey (Story-Builds.com) formatted the manuscript for publication and provided other valuable consultation.

Words cannot express my infinite and eternal gratitude to each of you. It takes a village to publish a decent book. Like everything else worthwhile in life, this is definitely a team effort.

FREE GIFT OFFER

At the time of this writing I offer a free, half-hour virtual "get acquainted" session which anyone can schedule through my website www.angelsabide.com. I'm happy to chat with you about the contents of this book or about other subjects as you wish.

If you are interested in gaining access to my virtual grief support groups, workshops, and retreats, I will give you details during our get acquainted session.

After the first free get acquainted session, my fees are fair, moderate, and flexible. My desire is to serve and support those who are honestly ready to move forward, regardless of their financial status.

Angels abide with you -

AUTHOR'S NOTE: A WORD
ABOUT WORDS

First, a word about *your* words. To receive the most benefit from this book you will do some journaling. Just put words on paper as honestly as you possibly can without editing or censoring. Don't be concerned about correct grammar, sentence or paragraph construction, handwriting, typographical errors, punctuation, or any of that... You cannot do this wrong as long as you are being honest with yourself.

At the end of each chapter, I have respectfully offered some questions for personal reflection, journaling, and/or for group discussion. These questions are simply prompts to get you started. Use the prompts or ignore them, but please put some of your thoughts and feelings down in writing if you wish to reach grief resolution.

If you decide to respond to some of the questions, there are *no wrong answers* and there are *no* trick questions. Whatever is true for you is valid. Over time you may want to respond to some of the questions more than once. Your perspective may change. You may want to date your writing to track how your thoughts and/or feelings evolve as you travel the spiral pathway of grief.

To receive the most benefit from this book, you will also find your grief companions. You may decide to selectively discuss some of your journaling with them at some point. However, don't be concerned about that as you are writing. Just write, then decide later how much of your journaling you discuss with others.

Chapter 6 is devoted entirely to helping your find your grief companions. Chapter 7 gives you citations for rigorous scientific research which has shown both journaling and participation in grief support groups to be effective in resolving grief.

Certainly you can use this book in any way that makes sense for you. You may want to read through it quickly the first time, start your journaling at any point, and then seek your grief companions. Once you find one or more companions, you can go back to some chapters of the book and continue your journaling and discussions.

You are not alone. I am available to assist and support you in your grief resolution process. You can schedule time with me by going to my website at www.angelsabide.com. The first half-hour "get acquainted" session is free. You can also send me email messages through the website.

Now about *my* words - In writing this book I have attempted to keep a tone that is more conversational than didactic. One way I've attempted to do this is to use contractions (for example, "isn't" instead of "is not"). I'm aware that until very recently the use of contractions in a manuscript was not considered appropriate. I hope my conversational tone is comfortable for my readers.

In keeping with the conversational tone, I generally refer to myself in the first person using the pronoun "I." Occasionally for no particular reason I switch to the more formal third person self-reference "your author." Remember the words of Ralph Waldo Emerson, the great American poet and transcendentalist philosopher who said, "A foolish consistency is the hobgoblin of little minds."

At the time of this writing, our English language in in transition. Collectively we are struggling to find ways to express ourselves clearly with more inclusive language.

For example, some writers including myself are not comfortable using masculine pronouns when referring to both males and females. This may mean we sometimes use other pronouns in a way that once would have been considered inappropriate and incorrect. At one time I would have objected to the use of pronouns the way I have used them here in this book. I'm finding that I prefer this newer style.

My professional social work education and training taught me to always view individuals in the context of various systems, including the family, the community, and the larger culture. This is reflected in my writing. I often mention "western industrialized culture" because it's important to be aware of the impact of culture on each of us. Otherwise, we are like the little fish who swam up to the big fish and said, "What is water?"

I sometimes use the term "spiritual beings on a human journey" to refer to humans. This comes from a quote attributed to Pierre Teilhard de Chardin, a French Jesuit priest, scientist, theologian, philosopher, and teacher, who said, *"We are not human beings having a spiritual experience. We are spiritual beings having a human experience."* I find this idea compelling and empowering. Your mileage may vary.

I'm open to feedback from my readers on these and other subjects. Feel free to contact me through my website: www. angelsabide.com.

PREFACE

Condolences and Congratulations

Beloved reader, I am guessing that you have experienced one or more painful losses or you would not be reading this book. Please accept my sincere condolences.

As someone who has experienced multiple traumatic losses, I empathize with the overwhelming, indescribably painful physical, emotional, and spiritual struggle which accompanies significant loss. This struggle affecting every area of our lives can be named with one word: grief.

In addition to offering my condolences, I also offer you my wholehearted congratulations. By reading this book you are reaching out for guidance and support. You are admitting that you don't know everything and demonstrating that you are willing to learn. This qualifies you as an exceptional human being. Reaching out takes extraordinary strength, wisdom, and courage. I applaud you and I pray to be worthy of your trust.

My own experiences with devastating grief in childhood and early adulthood motivated me to become a student of grief and then a teacher of grief education. I consciously sought to learn from grief and I actively sought out those who could help me. Now, even as I continue to learn, I consciously reach out for opportunities to pass forward the kindness that was shown to me.

Spirit led me to amazingly brilliant therapists, as well as to authors of very influential books, dynamic workshop/retreat leaders, plus many who were my peers in self-help groups. I needed multiple helpers and sources of guidance for years. I believe most of us can benefit from multiple learning opportunities and modes.

A professional social worker for the past forty years, my sensitivity to loss and grief made me aware that every client I've ever known has experienced traumatic loss – some through the death of significant others, some through

- divorce,
- trauma
- abandonment,
- abuse,
- betrayal,
- rejection,
- relocation,
- disillusionment,
- disability,
- addiction,
- natural disasters,
- miscarriage,
- health crises,
- unemployment, bankruptcy, or other financial reverses,
- pet loss,
- incarceration,
- estrangement,
- disfigurement and
- combinations of the above and/or
- other heartbreaking life events.

Working from my own lived experience with loss, my formal education and post-graduate continuing professional education, I integrated grief education and grief support into my work with clients whether the setting was medical social work, a mental health agencies, a substance abuse treatment program, geriatric social work, or private practice. One of my spiritual teachers, Edwene Gaines, says, "We teach best what we most need to learn."

For a time I was a full-time bereavement counselor for a large hospice care provider on the west coast of Florida. In that position I made three-to-five bereavement home visits every weekday following the deaths of our hospice patients. I made dozens of bereavement phone calls every week to families of our recently deceased patients. I also worked with individuals and families from the community who did not have patients under hospice care, but requested bereavement support. I facilitated weekly grief support groups and community grief education workshops. I absolutely loved the work with my families.

For several years I worked in the funeral industry as a Family Services Counselor. I helped families pre-plan their end-of-life care and also assisted families at the time of their need for funeral services. It was intense and very rewarding work.

As an ordained interfaith minister I have had the privilege of officiating at a number of funerals. I normally decline to officiate at weddings unless I have a personal connection with the bridal pair. But I never turn down an opportunity to officiate at a funeral. I find this to be very rewarding and meaningful.

On many occasions I have been a provider of continuing professional education classes on the subject of grief and effective grief support. In a death-denying, pain avoidant culture such as we've created in the Western industrialized world, even professional helpers (social workers, healthcare workers, clergy, funeral service providers, educators, first responders, and others) are usually not taught anything about grief in their required courses of study beyond a superficial, outdated, inaccurate lecture on stage theory (i.e., "the stages of grief are ...).

The professionals who attend continuing education events about grief and effective grief support will admit that they are attending the event as much for personal reasons as for professional reasons. I usually give the same basic presentation to professional groups as I give to lay or community groups. The helping professionals typically do not know any more about grief than lay people.

This book has evolved from presentations I have offered to both lay groups and to professional groups on grief resolution and integration (to be defined and described in subsequent chapters). In writing and publishing it I have three goals:

1. First and foremost, to offer hope to those who struggle with grief, along with a clearly marked map to reach grief resolution and integration;

2. To correct at least twenty common misunderstandings about grief;

3. To pass forward the care that has been shown to me.

To offer hope, I'll begin with this story about Abraham Lincoln, who has been a favorite historical figure of mine since my studious childhood. Throughout his lifetime he experienced what some might say was more than his share of grief. When he was a child several members of his family died, including his mother, a younger brother, and an older sister. He was estranged from his father.

As a young man, his fiancée became ill and died suddenly. In 1862, after being elected president, his beloved twelve-year-old son died of typhoid fever. Those who knew him personally reported that he seemed to grieve the injury and death of every soldier on the Civil War battlefield, whether the soldier wore the blue or the gray. At one point he wrote, "If what I feel were equally distributed to the whole human family, there would not be one cheerful face on earth."

The same year his son died, one of his dearest friends died in battle. Without using the word hope, he speaks of it eloquently in a thoughtful and sensitive condolence letter he wrote to the daughter of his fallen friend:

"...In this sad world of ours, sorrow comes to all, and it often comes with bitter agony. Perfect relief is not possible, except with time. You cannot now believe that you will ever feel better. But this is not true. You are sure to be happy again. Knowing this, truly believing it, will make you less miserable now. I have had enough experience to make this statement. ..."

If Abraham Lincoln could say this in the middle of the Civil War, shortly after the death of his own child and his dear friend, surely there is hope for the rest of us. There is hope in this idea: *we do not have to carry the pain of grief (or any other pain) to our graves... and we don't have to manage the pain alone.*

Later in this book I will offer simple, practical definitions of the terms "grief resolution" and "grief integration." I will describe this whole process of releasing pain and receiving comfort in great detail so that anyone who is willing to release grief and receive comfort can do so. *I give you my solemn word.*

Spiritual beings on a human journey are equipped with the innate ability to express and release painful emotional energies like those associated with grief in ways that are harmless, healing and cleansing. Having released the pain and created empty space in and around our hearts, we then have the ability to accept positive energy into that space in a way that is miraculously comforting and empowering.

If you doubt the idea of innate human ability to express and release painful emotional energy, consider this – healthy newborn babies are quite capable of eloquently expressing and releasing discomfort, irritation, impatience, hunger, fear, and other painful physical and emotional states. They are also quite proficient at allowing soothing comfort and nurturance to soak into their little hearts, souls and bodies to create an internal state of bliss. Human babies are born knowing how to do both.

Unfortunately, most children in western industrialized culture are taught early to dissociate from this innate wisdom and hide or repress painful emotions, rather than honestly expressing and releasing that energy. Once they survive infancy many are also taught to reject, resist or deflect comfort and nurturance.

In learning to grieve through to integration and resolution, we reclaim the wisdom with which we were born. By doing so, we build resilience, enhance our emotional and spiritual maturity, improve our ability help others, and increase our capacity for joy.

YOU were born knowing how to express and release pain and how to internalize caring and comfort. I will help you remember.

Loss and grief are among the most common of human experiences. In an ideal world,

- our families,
- schools,
- clergy and congregants from our houses of worship,
- co-workers and management at our workplaces,
- first responders,
- health care providers,
- social service providers,
- neighbors and the larger community,
- and even our government

would be equipped with knowledge and skills to respond in a compassionate and helpful manner when people inevitably experience traumatic loss and grief.

Unfortunately, we as a society are not yet at that level of maturity. However, I dream a world where collectively we *know* and *do* much better. Any individual can make a difference in their circles of influence and in the collective consciousness.

Will you join me in dreaming this dream? Learning and teaching together, this dream is attainable in our lifetimes, at least in our little corner of the world.

We can bring about change not only in our own circles of influence but in the world, one person at a time, if we are willing to do our own grief work. The term "grief work" means feeling the feelings rather than denying and repressing them, releasing the emotional energy harmlessly, then accepting love and light to fill up the resulting empty space around our hearts. Farther into this text, you will find detailed chapters with clear and simple instructions for doing your grief work.

NOTE: For a complete explanation of how healing ourselves as individuals has a meaningful positive impact on raising the collective consciousness of the entire human family, read the Introduction of my previous book *Ten Simple Strategies for a Happier You: Changing the World from the Inside Out* available on amazon.com in paperback and e-book formats.

Moving forward - first we will consider *why* misinformation and confusion about grief flourishes in our world. Then we will examine and correct twenty common misunderstandings about grief which are pervasive in western industrialized culture.

In the process we will learn the truth about grief as opposed to the half-truths, falsehoods and flat-out lies most of us are taught. Learning the truth about grief is the first strategy for resolving and integrating grief. This will lay the foundation for our later discussion of additional simple but powerful strategies that bring freedom and serenity to the bereaved.

Again, my most sincere condolences for your losses and my most sincere congratulations on the wisdom, courage and strength that brought you to here. I am honored to be your companion on this journey.

Take a deep breath, let it out, and repeat. As you read, remember to breathe, breathe, and breathe – inhale and exhale - slowly and deeply especially if your reading brings any intense emotions to your awareness. This may or may not happen. If it does happen, pause, breathe, and release through your breathing.

The intense emotional response will pass quickly if you just keep breathing and releasing. There is no reason to be afraid if this happens. If your feelings were going to kill you, you would already be dead. ...but you survived. Your best years are to come, if you follow the simple but powerful suggestions I offer you here.

For Personal Reflection, Journaling and Group Discussion

1. Review the list of heartbreaking human experiences which can result in grief. Which of these have you experienced? Are there other losses you've experienced that are not on the list?
2. What is your reaction to the quote by Abraham Lincoln? Would you agree or disagree with his thought?
3. What is your reaction to this thought: "We can bring about change not only in our own circles of influence but in the world, one person at a time, if we are willing to do our own grief work...."
4. "The term 'grief work' means feeling the feelings rather than denying and repressing them, releasing the emotional energy harmlessly, then accepting love and light to fill up the resulting empty space around our hearts...." Define "grief work" in your own words.

PART I

LEARNING THE TRUTH ABOUT GRIEF

CHAPTER 1

FALSEHOODS, HALF-TRUTHS,
AND FLAT-OUT LIES

Why are so many falsehoods, half-truths, and flat-out lies told and believed about grief?

My theory is based on a life-time of personal and professional experiences and observations. As I disclose my thoughts on this subject, please believe that *not one word is meant as criticism or blame of anyone or anything.* We are where we are in our collective consciousness as a culture, each of us doing our best with the challenges we've faced and the resources we have available.

My only intention is to shed light, instill hope, provide additional resources and options, and alleviate unnecessary suffering. I also wish to pass forward kindness and wisdom that has generously been given to me to help me in my grief journey.

So, why such confusion?

First, western industrialized culture historically is steeped in patriarchy, the rule of the male and the masculine. Fortunately, in recent years there has been a shift toward a healthier balance of shared power between the masculine and the feminine.

There has also been resistance and push-back to the shift toward a healthier balance. At best we collectively move two steps forward and one step back. Perhaps this is for the best. Too much cultural change too quickly, even if for the better, could be difficult to handle.

In any event, the values and vestiges of patriarchy are still very influential in our culture. These include a bias toward the rational and logical which are considered masculine and a disdain for the emotional, which is associated with the feminine aspect and therefore considered less valuable in a patriarchy. Grief is by definition intensely emotional and is therefore most commonly associated with the supposedly (but not truly) inferior feminine aspect.

Throughout my own childhood and young adult years, I have observed boys being trained to "be strong" and show no sadness, fear, or regret, which is considered weakness. I have heard young boys who show these feelings called "sissies" and "crybabies" and heard them being told "big boys don't cry."

I have heard men who express these feelings called "girly men" and have heard them ridiculed them for being effeminate – typically one of the worst things a male child, adolescent, or adult can be labeled in a patriarchal culture.

I'd like to think that such blatant emotional and verbal abuse is less common in more recent years among younger generations. My impression is that we still have room for improvement in this particular area.

There are still many who think tears are a sign of weakness and a loss of control, whether the one shedding tears is male or female. The illusion of control is highly valued in a patriarchy and any time a male or a female appears to "lose control" of emotions by expressing them in any way that shows vulnerability, we consider this a character failure and a weakness. When people cry, some say they "broke down."

I have repeatedly heard people describe themselves on occasions when despite their concentrated efforts they started crying in public. They say, "I just lost it...." I believe they usually mean that they lost control of their emotions which resulted in tears.

Depending on the situation and my relationship with the person, I have sometimes said to them, "It sounds to me like you found it." What I mean is that in the moment the person found and expressed the emotional truth, which I consider a good thing.

This shaming of tears and all other normal outward signs of grief considered effeminate and womanish leads to suppression and silencing of mourning practices that could be very beneficial to individuals, families, communities, and our entire nation. In an atmosphere of shaming, suppression, and silencing, false information abounds.

Healthy fully functioning humans, both males and females, can think logically and also can feel their feelings and express them appropriately. Perhaps someday both the intellectual and the emotional functions of all humans will be equally accepted, valued and nurtured in our culture.

You and I can dream together of a world where men and women, boys and girls, use their good minds and rational, logical powers and are also free to respond to life with appropriate emotions without being shamed or ridiculed. In the meantime, we can choose to be counterculture in our own individual lives by creating within ourselves a working complementary balance of thinking and feeling.

We can individually create this healthy internal balance whether we are males or females. We can bring that new world into existence, one person at a time, until we literally change the culture. I will teach you how to be a part of that healing transformation if you are willing to learn.

NOTE: If you would like a detailed explanation of how individual transformation leads to evolution of the collective consciousness, see my book *"Ten Simple Strategies for a Happier You: Changing the World from the Inside Out,* available in paperback and e-book formats on Amazon.com.

Another reason there is so much misunderstanding about grief is that grief is often inaccurately associated only with physical death. ...and as a culture we deny death. This has been documented thoroughly and repeatedly. If you have any doubt that this is true, do a quick internet search on the term "death denying culture" and/or simply bring up the subjects of death and grief in one or more personal or professional conversations and watch the reaction.

. . .

GRIEF CAN RESULT from any traumatic loss, whether the loss is a

- physical death,
- a divorce,
- a disability,
- a disfigurement,
- a miscarriage,
- a trauma of any kind,
- a downsizing, unemployment, or other financial reverses,
- an estrangement,
- an incarceration,
- a relocation,

OR EVEN THE loss of intangibles, such as the following:

- delusions (e.g., "My child would *never* use illegal drugs,")
- cherished illusions (e.g., "If I only try hard enough, I can control...."),
- dreams,
- hopes,
- faith,
- or others.

Anything that results in the loss of normalcy triggers grief.

Our collective denial of death has expanded into an avoidance of all things closely associated with death, including grief. So we avoid acknowledging death and its close associate, grief. *When we avoid talking about and otherwise deny something, misinformation multiplies exponentially.*

Another reason there is so much confusion around grief is that in addition to being a death denying culture, ours is a pain avoidant culture. This is less well documented but nevertheless apparent to any observer. Pain of any kind is considered unacceptable, intolerable and to be evaded at any cost. In particular, emotional pain is to be medicated, repressed or ignored.

To admit being in emotional pain, even after a traumatic loss, is considered shameful. "Keep a stiff upper lip and get off your pity pot. ... Get over it and move on" is considered an appropriate answer to any admission of feeling sad or afraid or vulnerable in any way – that message or religious platitudes or abruptly changing the subject. Later I will offer some more appropriate, compassionate, empathetic responses.

One last reason there is so much confusion around the reality of grief is the legacy of patriarchal shame/fear/guilt-based religion. Bear with me and please don't assume that I am "anti-religion." I am not. However, I'm acutely aware that many of my baby-boomer generation as well as younger generations have rejected the dogma of traditional interpretations of religion but have never explored and discovered a practical alternative; that is, a non-shaming belief system that works (what a concept!)

Americans claiming "no religion" are sometimes referred to as "nones" because of how they answer the question "what is your religious tradition?" According to 2019 General Social Survey data, "nones" now represent about 23.1 percent of the population – almost one in four! In fact, "nones" are reported to be the single fastest growing religious (or non-religious) group in the United States. The percentage of people answering "none" has shown a constant, steady increase since the beginning of the new millennium.

There are also those who are called "dones." At one time they were active in organized religious life but for various reasons have become inactive and have no plan to ever resume participation in organized religion. They are done.

There are also active members of various religious groups who doubt the teachings of the group (usually keeping their doubts to themselves) and/or doubt if they themselves are "good enough" to receive grace.

Many of the nones, the dones, and the doubters decided what they *don't* believe but never determined what they *do* believe instead. Again, the culture does not support or reward the on-going exploration, reflection, and study necessary to develop an authentic, personal belief system.

NOTE: Anyone who wishes to explore the difference between religion and non-shaming spirituality and learn ways to joyfully celebrate your inherent spirituality, see the chapter on spirituality in my book *"Ten Simple Strategies for a Happier You: Changing the World from the Inside Out,"* available on Amazon.com in paperback and e-book formats. Anyone who is interested in reading about spirituality or religion might enjoy this chapter, but it might be especially interesting to those who consider themselves "spiritual but not religious."

Under extreme stress, such as that created by traumatic loss, people often regress into a vulnerable, childlike state of mind. They may have developed the ability to keep that inner child hidden from public view, but they may be constantly or intermittently flooded with the distress of that childlike part of themselves.

Time is an abstraction that children do not comprehend. Children only know the present moment. If the present moment is painful, it feels as if the pain will never end. When adults are regressed into a childlike state of consciousness and they are flooded with pain, it seems the pain will last forever.

In a regressed state, bereaved adults often default to either the shame/fear/guilt-based dogma taught to them in childhood or to toxic ideas absorbed by osmosis in western patriarchy – shame-based concepts about God, the purpose and meaning of life, death, the afterlife and other mysteries. When this happens, they often experience intense fear, sadness, shame, guilt and confusion.

Not knowing what else to do or where to turn, they repress those feelings. Except for fleeting thoughts of "What did I do to deserve this?" or "Why is God punishing me like this?" or just "Why ...?" they never engage in the contemplation, reflection, study and support required to make meaning of the loss.

Unfortunately, many self-medicate the painful emotions, which is commonly accepted and encouraged in our culture. Rather than express and release emotional pain, many people learn to anesthetize themselves with a combination of mood-altering substances and compulsive behaviors, including but not limited to:

- alcohol,
- prescription or illegal drugs,
- food, especially refined carbohydrates, called comfort food,
- work,
- busy-ness,
- addictive relationships,
- gambling,
- sex,
- shopping, called retail therapy,
- religiosity,
- exercise and sports,
- and others.

Almost anything and everything can be used to distract grieving people from the pain of loss if they have no internal permission to express and release the pain and no support for that process. Obviously, when emotional pain is repressed and self-medicated, it is not released and healed. It is merely hidden to some degree. It does not go away.

Those who become really practiced at distracting themselves and self-medicating can get so good at it that they are not even aware they are doing it. They hide emotional pain even from themselves. Unfortunately, when taken to extremes, the substances and compulsive behaviors most effective at medicating emotional pain can create complications much more difficult to resolve than grief. The pain gets trapped in the body, mind, soul and spirit and can lead to serious mental, emotional, and spiritual illness.

Internalized, unresolved grief *which is not properly attended* can mutate into

- clinical depression,
- panic and anxiety disorders,
- substance and/or behavioral addictions,

- suicidal thoughts and behaviors, and
- other life-threatening mental health challenges.

It can also trigger a huge variety of life-limiting physical illnesses including but not limited to

- heart and vascular diseases,
- diabetes,
- cancer,
- autoimmune disorders,
- musculoskeletal diseases,
- gastrointestinal disorders,
- painful disfiguring skin conditions,
- and many others.

To be clear, I am not suggesting that these physical and mental health challenges are all caused by grief and only grief. I'm suggesting that unresolved grief can be a significant contributing factor to these conditions.

I firmly believe that the great majority of citizens of the modern developed western world are carrying within their hearts, minds, bodies and souls huge burdens of unattended grief. I also believe that many of our chronic physical and mental health concerns are directly related to unattended grief.

When grief is properly attended, enormous positive results are realized. Some even experience what is now called "post-traumatic growth." When grief is denied, shamed, and repressed, negative consequences are the inevitable result. Absolutely no good comes from repressing grief indefinitely.

My own beloved father had no internal permission to express and release painful emotions which might reveal vulnerability. He could express anger but he never released it.

He started smoking cigarettes at age 12 and by adulthood he smoked two packs a day. He was a workaholic, working seven days a week, many hours each day.

He became a heart patient in his thirties. He refused to follow a heart healthy food plan. He tried but was never able to stop smoking cigarettes. He had quadruple by-pass surgery at age 50 and very serious aneurysm surgery at age 56.

After his by-pass surgery he became much more emotional and expressive than he had ever been. When we had opportunities to visit, at the end of the visit he would always become tearful. He would then become embarrassed and struggle to choke back his tears.

At age 58, he was still straight and tall, with dark hair gray at the temples, brilliant blue eyes and a cleft in his chin. When he dropped dead of a heart attack, he left a beautiful corpse.

I believe with all my heart that he died of unshed tears, unspoken fears, and unforgiven resentments. Over thirty years later, I still miss him.

To be very clear – grief is *not* an illness of any kind. It is *not* a mental illness, a spiritual illness, or an emotional illness. *Grief only becomes problematic when the grieving person is shamed and/or pressured to hide their feelings*, which unfortunately is the most common experience with grief in western industrialized culture.

By repressing the uncomfortable feelings of grief, we also limit our capacity for the more pleasant feelings of joy, serenity, gratitude, empathy, and love. Those who do not receive the permission and support to integrate grief miss a life-enhancing opportunity to grow into more spiritually and emotionally mature people. They miss the opportunity to learn how to be of real comfort to others who grieve.

Beloved reader, it does not have to be this way. Grief can be normalized so that those who experience loss - and that would include all of us sooner or later - have permission and support to express painful feelings and release them harmlessly. Those who mourn can be showered with loving support to fill those empty spaces in the heart. Then, when they're ready, they can pass forward the permission and the support to others.

Truly, grief is a symptom of health. Only relatively healthy people have the ability to form healthy relationships and connections. When these relationships and connections are disrupted, the painful disruption is called grief.

I heard once that grief is the price we pay for loving. The idea stayed with me; it seems to me to be true.

Before I move forward into identifying and refuting twenty common misunderstandings about grief, let me repeat for emphasis: *absolutely nothing I write is intended as criticism or blame of anyone or anything.* I simply describe what I see and experience and call it like I see it. *Take what is helpful and leave the rest.*

We are where we are as a culture. My hope and intention is to help all of us move forward to greater and greater health and happiness. While mentioning western industrialized patriarchal culture, I want to be clear that *I absolutely love my country.* While it is inhabited by imperfect human beings like myself and therefore is far from perfect, I have never seriously considered living anywhere else.

I could write a book about the advantages and benefits of living in the U.S.A. Perhaps one day I will. For now, I feel called to write this one. I am hopeful that this book can help the citizens of the United States and the entire western industrialized world to collectively move a step closer to realizing the lofty ideals upon which this country was established.

For Personal Reflection, Journaling and Group Discussion

1. "...the values ... of patriarchy ...include a bias toward the rational and logical which are considered masculine and a disdain for the emotional, which is associated with the feminine aspect and therefore considered less valuable in a patriarchy. Grief is by definition intensely emotional and is therefore most commonly associated with the supposedly (but not truly) inferior feminine aspect." What is your reaction to this statement?

2. *"You and I can dream together of a world where men and women, boys and girls, use their good minds and rational, logical powers and are also free to respond to life with appropriate emotions without being shamed or ridiculed."* Your response?

3. " ...ours is a pain avoidant culture. ... Pain of any kind is considered unacceptable, intolerable and to be evaded at any cost." Your response?

4. "...many of my baby-boomer generation as well as younger generations have rejected the dogma of traditional interpretations of religion but have never explored and discovered a practical alternative; that is, a non-shaming belief system that works..." Your response?

5. "...Almost anything and everything can be used to distract grieving people from the pain of loss if they have no internal permission to express and release the pain and no support for that process...." Review the list of common substances and behaviors used to medicate emotional pain. Which of these have you used to medicate emotional pain?

6. Referring to my father, I write, "*I believe with all my heart that he died of unshed tears, unspoken fears, and unforgiven resentments.*" Do you know of anyone who may have died prematurely of unshed tears, unspoken fears, and unforgiven resentments?

7. "...grief is a symptom of health..." Your response?

CHAPTER 2

MOST COMMON, DAMAGING GRIEF FALSEHOOD

FALSE: There are five *stages* of grief ending in acceptance and therefore (by implication) grief is much the same for everyone, predictable, self-limiting, finite, and linear. ....and if I reach acceptance, I will lose all connection with that beloved someone I have lost.

This could actually be considered seven falsehoods and we will consider each of the seven separately in this chapter.

With all due respect to Dr. Elizabeth Kubler-Ross, this pervasive idea of "five stages of grief ending in acceptance" is a half-truth at best. A brilliant, visionary Swiss-American psychiatrist born in 1926, Dr. Kubler-Ross published her book *On Death and Dying* in the early 1960's after interviewing over 200 hospitalized terminally ill patients, many of them more than once. The book became an international best-seller.

When she published the findings of her interviews, she brought death and dying out of the closet and gave permission and support for medical professionals and lay persons alike to discuss death openly. This was a HUGE breakthrough and for this and other notable professional achievements we owe Dr. Kubler-Ross appreciation and honor for her priceless contributions to thanatology.

Her book included the "five stages" as they related to the process of dying. Unfortunately, her work was misinterpreted, generalized and misapplied to the grief process. Western patriarchal culture grabbed onto the idea of "five stages of grief" and ran away with it. This was a convenient way to make the rather messy, highly emotional subject of grief less scary, less awkward, and altogether more tidy, logical and rational. Grief suddenly became more masculine and less emotional and "womanish."

Dr. Kubler-Ross, or Elizabeth as I like to think of her, authored twenty additional books before she died in 2004. She finished her work on her last book titled *On Grief and Grieving: Finding the Meaning of Grief Through the Five Stages of Loss,*" just months before she died. It was published in 2005 after her death.

The Author's Note, signed by both Elizabeth and her co-author David Kessler, appears before the preface and states, "There is no correct way or time to grieve. We wrote this book hoping to familiarize the reader with the *aspects* of grief and grieving..." (Italics added.) The first chapter of the book is titled "The Five Stages of Grief: Denial, Anger, Bargaining, Depression, and Acceptance," and begins with these words (Italics added):

"The stages have evolved since their introduction, and *they have been misunderstood over the past three decades. They were never meant to help tuck messy emotions into neat packages.* They are responses to loss that many people have, *but there is not a typical response to loss, as there is no typical loss. ...*" A few pages into the first chapter comes this admission, "The stages of loss...have been widely used and misused."

I appreciate Elizabeth's attempt to clarify her stage theory and her acknowledgment that the stages had been misunderstood and misused (her exact words). However, by the time this last book was published there had been almost forty years for the misunderstandings about the five stages to become deeply embedded in the collective consciousness of western culture.

Her last book has not yet been nearly as influential as her first – and in her last book she refers to *"The Five Stages of Loss"* in her subtitle, in the title of the first chapter and throughout the text of the book! While Elizabeth is not responsible for the way her work has been misapplied, my wish is that she had done more in her lifetime to challenge its misinterpretation and misuse.

In her first book and in her last book, I find the use of the word "stages" to be unfortunate. I wish she had used some other word (perhaps the word "aspects" as in the Author's Note to her final book) in the subtitle and in the text of the final book. I wish she had more strongly emphasized the individuality of the grief journey. While the original theory did some good, it also created some adverse repercussions.

In spite of these concerns, I honor her genius and I don't use that word lightly. During her time, Elizabeth personally trained hundreds of medical students and professional colleagues. Through her publications, she has greatly influenced subsequent generations to humanize medical care for the dying. Through her work, she greatly reduced the stigma associated with terminal illness and pioneered the modern hospice movement. I appreciate the foundation she laid for all of us.

One good thing that came from the mistaken notion of "stages of grief" is that when people heard the stages of grief named (denial, anger, depression, bargaining, and acceptance), they heard validation and permission to be in denial for a time and to feel anger and sadness. For many this was the first time in their lives they had received such validation and permission. For many this was the first time since experiencing traumatic loss.

Here are my concerns about the adverse repercussions resulting from the misuse of stage theory.

Saying that the "stages" end in acceptance sounds good and gives people hope. Hope is a good thing, but only when it is based on reality. False hope is not helpful and the idea that there are five stages of grief ending in acceptance gives false hope.

"The five stages of grief ending in acceptance" has been interpreted by many to mean that if the grieving person just waits for an unspecified period of time they will reach acceptance without any conscious effort. That's not how it happens. The only way anyone reaches anything resembling acceptance is by engaging in the type of active, intentional grief work described in detail in future chapters.

By teaching the "five stages of grief ending in acceptance," the implication is that grief is much the same for everyone, predictable, self-limiting, finite, and linear. Truly, it's none of these.

These erroneous ideas lead only to confusion, guilt, and feelings of inadequacy. Countless people have told me with great embarrassment and distress that they must not be grieving correctly because they are not following the prescribed order of the five stages and have not yet mastered acceptance. More about this in just a few pages.

There are other concerns with stage theory and many highly credentialed professionals have thoughtfully challenged it. For example, numerous writers have observed that there is no data-based evidence that most people most of the time go through most of the stages of grief in the order commonly presented or in any other order.

One such clinician is Russell P. Friedman, executive director of the Grief Recovery Institute in Sherman Oaks, Calif. (www.grief-recovery.com), and co-author of *The Grief Recovery Handbook* (HarperCollins, 1998), who wrote

> *"no study has ever established that stages of grief actually exist, and what are defined as such can't be called stages.... No matter how much people want to create simple, bullet-point guidelines for the human emotions of grief, there are no stages of grief that fit any two people or relationships."* (Italics added.)

University of Memphis psychologist Robert A. Neimeyer confirms this analysis. He concluded in his scholarly book *Meaning Reconstruction and the Experience of Loss* (American Psychological Association, 2001): "...scientific studies have failed to support any discernible sequence of emotional phases of adaptation to loss or to identify any clear end point to grieving that would designate a state of 'recovery.'"

NOTE: For a more thorough review of scholarly work that refutes the stages theory of grief, do an internet search using the search words "debunking five stages of grief" or "refuting Elizabeth Kubler-Ross' five stages of grief."

Remember, Elizabeth did her research by interviewing

hospitalized terminally ill patients about their experience. After receiving permission from the patients' attending physician, she approached the patients and asked if they would help her learn to improve care for seriously ill people. With few exceptions they agreed.

Elizabeth visited repeatedly those who agreed to help her and asked insightful open-ended questions without preconception as to the correct answers. Colleagues who knew her have described Elizabeth as highly intuitive and empathetic. She listened attentively to the patients. She responded without judgment and respected the patient's boundaries. She did not push them to disclose beyond their comfort levels. She was clear with them that she was most interested in hearing about their state of mind and/or their emotional experience since they received their terminal diagnoses.

In researching *On Death and Dying*, Dr. Kubler-Ross noticed certain patterns in the patients' emotional preparations for death as they neared the end of their lives. These patterns became known as "the stages of dying" and then, erroneously, "the stages of grief." Under the extraordinary circumstances of her interviews, the majority of Elizabeth's terminally ill subjects reached a degree of acceptance and peace before they died.

Tragically, many of us in western culture never reach any level of acceptance and serenity regarding our losses, partly because most of us have little or no experience with a non-judgmental, empathetic, intuitive listener. Most people are not good listeners because they have so rarely (if ever) enjoyed the experience of having a good listener's undivided attention for any meaningful period of time. The obvious exception would be those extraordinarily wise people who have invested in professional therapy.

While few of us may ever develop the communication and rapport-building skills Elizabeth demonstrated, any of us can become comfortable attending to another person's grief in a way that makes a positive difference. The most important requirement for becoming a skilled grief companion is that we must first do our own grief work so that we can give our full attention to the person we want to support.

Otherwise, we can easily become flooded with our own grief

while we are attempting to comfort another. Then the newly bereaved person feels guilty and embarrassed for upsetting the one who is attempting to give comfort. When this happens, everyone just feels worse and typically vows never to attempt such a conversation again.

NOTE: If you are interested in providing care and comfort that makes a difference to others who grieve, I will teach you how to do that by following the suggestions later in this book. *I PROMISE!*

So back to the flat-out lies that are implied by "the stages of grief ending in acceptance," specifically the falsehoods that grief is 1) much the same for everyone, 2) predictable, 3) self-limiting, 4) finite, and 5) linear.

To refute each of these implied falsehoods individually:

FIRST, *grief is NOT the same for everyone. In fact, grief is as unique as a fingerprint.* Every person's grief journey is unique, depending on a multitude of factors, including but not limited to:

- the gender of the person grieving,
- the birth order of the griever in their family of origin,
- the nature of the loss (whether it is personal, material, abstract, concrete, small, medium, large, etc.),
- the family and community culture of the one grieving,
- the history of the griever and their past experience with traumatic loss,
- the griever's past experience with grief support,
- the availability and accessibility of emotional and spiritual support,
- the temperament of the griever (introvert or extrovert, whether they typically react first with thinking or typically react first with feeling, whether they tend more toward abstract or concrete thinking, etc.).

Some will experience intensely all of the feelings mentioned in the traditional five stages of grief plus other feelings Dr. Kubler-Ross never mentioned. Some may experience only one or two predominant feelings much less intensely. Some will have a great need to talk about the loss and others will have less need to talk. Other variables are apparent to any open-minded observer.

What's important to remember is that there is no one correct way to grieve. In fact, I submit that we cannot grieve incorrectly. There are ways to process grief that are more likely to be life-enhancing. We will discuss much more about this in later chapters. There are ways to grieve that may ultimately be self-defeating and may have detrimental consequences. However, *no one* benefits when criticized for failing to grieve according to a prescribed formula or schedule. Sadly, I've known of multiple instances of this happening.

Each person's timeline for grief can vary greatly. David B. Feldman, Ph.D. is a professor at Santa Clara University, author, speaker, and host of the popular 'Psychology in 10 Minutes' podcast. According to Feldman, moving through stages isn't how grief actually works.

"The five stages have normalized strong emotions during times of loss," Feldman said, "but they don't really capture every experience a person can have. ...(and) it really isn't the case that most people spend two weeks in denial, two weeks in anger, two weeks in bargaining... *Instead, people cycle through these experiences at all different speeds....*" (Italics added.)

Many years ago, I met a lovely woman I'll call Pam to protect her privacy. She was in her mid-fifties at the time we met and became acquainted. Pam was the oldest of six siblings. Her father was a career military officer. Pam was in her early twenties and had recently married when her mother became ill and died.

Shortly after his wife's death, Pam's father accepted an assignment in Europe and left several of his children (Pam's younger siblings) in Pam's care. With what would have been an impossible caregiving task for many, Pam had plenty to distract her. She did not have the luxury of healthy grief.

She realized thirty years after the fact that she had never grieved for her mother. The grief had not gone away, although it had long been ignored. When I met her, Pam had recently started participating in a hospice grief support group. She wisely sought the safety and comfort of the grief group in order to attend to her long-neglected emotional needs. I admired her courage, strength, and wisdom.

It's never too late to do grief work. It's never too early to prepare for life's inevitable shocks and curve balls. ...and we don't have to do it alone.

While every grief experience is as unique as a fingerprint, in one way every grief experience is the same. *Every grief experience is by definition intensely emotional.* So everyone's grief experience is unique and everyone's grief experience is the same.

Fred Rogers, an ordained minister and the creator, composer, writer, puppeteer, and host of public television's *Mister Rogers' Neighborhood* said, "As different as we are from one another, as unique as each one of us is, we are much more the same than we are different. ..."

Some people feel their emotions more intensely than others, but everyone has *relatively* intense emotional responses to significant loss. When I use the word "relatively" in this context, I mean that everyone has *what is for them* intense emotional responses to loss. What seems very intense to one person may not be so intense to another.

Thankfully, we are not in competition for a prize or award given to the one who suffers most or least. Everyone suffers some degree of emotional distress in grief, but we can all suffer less if we believe the truth about grief and actively, intentionally do our grief work. As promised before, a complete detailed description of active and intentional grief work follows in later chapters.

SECOND, grief is not predictable, as implied by the concept of "five stages of grief ending in acceptance." I've heard grief described as a roller coaster. I would say that grief is the only roller coaster that not only goes up and down and upside down in nauseating loop-de-loops but can also suddenly jerk to a sudden stop and reverse directions without any warning or discernible pattern. Now the passengers are all hurtling backwards at terrifying speeds!

A person can actively grieve and reach a degree of true acceptance and serenity and can be sailing along smoothly creating their new normal. Suddenly, out of nowhere a scent, a song, a date on the calendar, another loss, a glimpse of a stranger in a public place who looks oddly familiar, a dream, or some other stimulus can trigger a tsunami of intense emotions.

It's almost as if the original loss just happened and we are back at ground zero. Again there is shock and possibly great sadness, anger, confusion, guilt, fear, hopelessness, and/or other intense feelings associated with loss. ... And we may be thinking something like, *"REALLY?? AGAIN??* I thought I was *through* all this!! What's *wrong* with me?? Am I *crazy??"*

I call this "re-cycling." It is normal and to be expected, but does not fit neatly into the "five stages of grief." Please know that with every re-cycling of grief, acceptance and serenity are integrated simultaneously at both *higher* and *deeper* levels of awareness. Over time, with conscious, active grief work, episodes of re-cycling become less and less frequent, less intensely painful, and of shorter and shorter duration. More about this later.

THIRD, grief is NOT self-limiting as one might expect from hearing "the five stages of grief ending in acceptance." As mentioned before, a grieving person does not reach acceptance automatically. *Arriving at serenity, acceptance and integration in relation to a traumatic loss requires conscious intention and conscientious grief work.*

Later I will describe clearly and carefully exactly what I mean by conscious intention and conscientious active grief work. I will give clear descriptions of exactly how to do this work. For now, trust me when I tell you that *grief work is something you can do successfully if you are willing* and you don't have to do it alone. I will help and there are others who are also available to help. I will help you find them.

FOURTH, grief is NOT finite, as implied by the wording "five stages of grief ending in acceptance." Finite means "relating to something with an end." Grief is *NOT* pre-set with a definite terminus, *NOT* fixed in time and space with a predetermined ending, *NOT* programmed by some great cosmic grief programmer to end at a specified finishing point.

Rather, grief is *open-ended* and *infinite*. Once we have experienced traumatic loss and significant grief, we are changed forever. We have no choice about that. There is no going back. Our only choice is how we respond.

Simply stated, we have two choices. We can either 1) learn from grief, becoming wiser and living more fully, or 2) we can avoid and repress grief, become numb to life with all its joys and sorrows, and risk becoming depressed, anxious, bitter, broken, and/or brittle.

We don't get over grief. We go *through* it and ideally, learn from it. The loss and the feelings associated with it are part of our history and at best become integrated into our lived experience.

Lest you despair, I remind you again that *with conscious intention and conscientious active grief work*, described carefully in later chapters, grief can soften and can be integrated in a way that allows for greater joy, serenity, affection, spiritual and emotional maturity, and gratitude for everyday pleasures and blessings – greater perhaps than you have ever known. This life-enhancement after a traumatic loss is sometimes called *"post-traumatic growth."* This is the promise and potential of grief *when grief is properly attended.*

His Holiness, the Dalai Lama, said it this way:

"When we meet real tragedy in life, we can react in two ways – either by losing hope and falling into self-destructive habits, or by using the challenge to find our inner strength."

FIFTH, grief is most certainly *not* a linear experience as one might expect from hearing "the five stages of grief ending in acceptance." Grief does not progress in one direction along a straight line. Revisiting the roller coaster analogy, no roller coaster runs on a straight track.

Imagine a spiral as a model of the grief pathway over time. Think of a slinky toy that stretches indefinitely in two directions at a forty-five degree angle. One end extends downward to the earth and the other end stretches upward to the heavens. Each curve of the spiral represents an occasion of expressing and releasing a layer of emotional pain from our hearts and receiving caring energy into the empty space. Every time this happens, the spiral extends one more curve upward or higher and simultaneously extends one more curve downward or deeper.

I've already mentioned the process of "re-cycling" grief issues. As it is happening, re-cycling the feelings of a traumatic loss can feel like a giant step backwards if one is unaware of the on-going nature of the grief process. In truth, re-cycling is part of the process of integration of grief at *simultaneously higher and deeper levels of awareness.*

Carl Sandburg, the Pulitzer-prize winning Swedish-American poet, said, "Life is like an onion. You peel it off one layer at a time, and sometimes you weep." To me this seems an accurate appraisal of life in general as well as an insightful description of the grief process in particular.

Grief gets repressed and packed down in layers in our bodies, hearts, and souls. When a re-cycling occurrence is triggered by that song, that scent, that date on the calendar, another loss, a dream, seeing that stranger in a crowd who looks familiar - or by any other stimulus - a deeper layer of grief has been brought to the surface to be expressed and harmlessly released. It's all part of the process of integration and it's a sign of health rather than a sign of failure or insanity.

No one can release all their grief in an instant and have it done once and for all time. We could not survive that. So within each of us is an exquisitely sensitive and highly intelligent mechanism that monitors what dose of grief we can withstand at any given moment in time. This Inner Wisdom allows only a tolerable level of pain to enter our conscious awareness at any particular point. We don't have to be afraid of the pain.

We experience that dose of pain and we integrate it when we:

1. breathe (inhale and exhale),
2. take one day or one hour or one minute or one moment at a time,
3. feel what we feel,
4. breathe,
5. express and
6. release our pain harmlessly and appropriately,
7. breathe,

8. receive comfort and support to fill the empty place created around our hearts when we released the pain,
9. breathe, and then
10. when we are ready, pass forward the comfort and support.

We knew how to do this the day we were born. With intentional practice this becomes routine and automatic on a day to day basis.

Over time we notice that in this process we have gradually become not only peaceful (most of the time), but stronger, softer, wiser, more resilient, more empathetic, more compassionate, and more spiritually mature human beings. This phenomenon has been called *post-traumatic growth*. Once we have achieved post-traumatic growth, we have the tools and skills we need to promptly re-establish our peaceful equilibrium any time we allow something or someone to disrupt our serenity.

Finally, there is one more damaging repercussion from the stage theories presented by Elizabeth and subsequent other writers. This applies only to grief associated with the death of a significant person and doesn't apply to grief associated with loss from causes other than death. (By the way, this is one of the few things in this book that applies *only* to grief from the death of a significant person. With very few obvious exceptions, everything else is applicable to grief resulting from any cause.)

Elizabeth's five stages ended in acceptance. Subsequent stage theorists described an ending or completion to grief which included "detachment" or "withdrawing emotional energy" from the deceased person, "moving on," "reaching closure," "letting go" and building a "new life" with "new relationships." *Many who have survived the death of a loved one do not want to reach acceptance if it means "detach, move on, let go, reach closure, and build a new life with new relationships."*

There is a widely believed implication that "... *if I reach acceptance about this death, I will lose all connection with that precious someone I have lost. My pain is the only thing that keeps me connected.*" This misunderstanding has caused untold numbers of bereaved persons to be stuck in the most painful depths of the grief process and has unnecessarily extended their acute suffering.

In stage theory literature there has been implied and even

blatant judgement for anyone who resists letting go completely of the past. Such resistance has been interpreted as dysfunctional to the point of being called pathological.

If you are not acquainted with the more recent "Continuing Bonds" theory of grief, I am happy to be the one to introduce you. In 1996, researchers Klass, Silverman, and Nickman published a book titled *"Continuing Bonds: New Understandings of Grief,"* which challenged the traditional stage or linear theories of grief.

The writers declared that healthy, normal resolution of grief does not require detachment or closure. Instead, they documented with numerous contributors that survivors of deceased loved ones can in time find meaningful ways to create a new relationship with the deceased and maintain positive continuing bonds.

This theory goes so far as to say that continuing bonds are not only NOT pathological, but an important part of healthy grief! The theorists use cross-cultural studies to show that *human attachment is natural even in death*.

Those who have been dear to us in this lifetime do not disappear from our hearts or from our memories. They are still a member of our biological or spiritual families. The bonds that transcend death endure in different ways and to varying degrees throughout the lifetime of the survivors as they mature and continue their lives on planet Earth.

There is an infinite variety of healthy positive ways we can maintain continuing bonds with our loved ones who have died, including for example,

- having pictures of them visible in our home,
- having conversations with them,
- writing letters or notes to them,
- sharing a positive memory of them,
- continuing a tradition that was important to them,
- lighting a candle in their honor on their birthdays/holidays/the anniversary of the death/anytime,
- doing our best to follow a good example they set for us,
- thinking about what good advice they might give us in a difficult situation,
- donating money to a good cause they supported,

- volunteering to support a good cause they believed in,
- planting a tree in their memory,
- donating a copy of one of their favorite books to the public library,
- using a special recipe they were known to have used,
- cherishing selected personal items of the deceased,
- starting a foundation or scholarship fund in their honor,
- visiting places where you feel closer to them,
- hanging special ornaments on a holiday tree in their memory,
- and others.

You can decide which if any of these or other actions would be most meaningful and comforting to you in maintaining positive bonds with a deceased loved one.

The following is a touching story of a man who maintained continuing bonds with his wife who died one day after giving birth to their daughter. According to Wikipedia,

In the spring of 2008, Matthew Logelin began using a personal blog to keep friends and family informed of his expectant wife's condition when she began hospital bed rest. Their daughter, Madeline, was born healthy, though seven weeks premature, on March 24, 2008. Mother and baby appeared to be doing well, but the very next day, Logelin's wife, Liz, suddenly collapsed and died of a pulmonary embolism while on the way to hold their newborn for the first time.

Logelin turned to his blog as an outlet for his grief, and a place to share his challenges and triumphs in raising a premature infant without his wife. As news of his wife's death spread, his readership began to grow, with commentators offering advice, encouragement, and sending care packages. In 2009, a group of these readers organized a 5K Walk/Run in memory of Liz Logelin, to be held on her birthday.

This first event, which would become an annual event in years to come, was dubbed The Liz Goodman Logelin Memorial 5K and brought in over $4,000. Though intended for Matt Logelin and his daughter, Logelin opted to instead donate the funds to many of the other widows and widowers he'd met through his blog, paving the way for the beginnings of The Liz Logelin Foundation.

"The Liz Logelin Foundation is a way to honor Liz, but it's much more than that," Logelin has said. "After Liz died, so many people reached out to help me, and I felt a responsibility to give back in a similar way. Starting a foundation seemed like the best way to do that."

The logo for the foundation carries a stargazer lily, his wife's favorite and the flower she chose for their wedding in 2005, as well as a pink font – her favorite color.

According to the website http://thelizlogelinfoundation.org, since its founding in 2009, The Liz Logelin Foundation has given grants to more than 160 families. You may never start a foundation, but hearing about just one person who did hopefully will inspire and motivate you to do what works for you to maintain comforting continuing bonds if you are grieving the death of a loved one.

So the powerful news is that we can express and release harmlessly any painful emotions associated with the loss and still maintain positive connections with our loved ones who have died. In a later chapter I will give you detailed suggestions as to how to express and harmlessly release the pain of grief so that only the positive continuing bonds are left in your heart.

There is one caution to keep in mind. If your relationship with the deceased was troubled and/or ambivalent while they were alive, the relationship has the potential to be troublesome in death. In this case, it would be appropriate to see a grief professional and be totally honest with them about the ambivalence and the troubling nature of the relationship both before and since the death. In a later chapter I will offer some guidelines for finding a suitable professional grief companion/mentor/guide/coach.

The 1996 book along with a follow-up (*Continuing Bonds in Bereavement: New Directions for Research and Practice,* compiled by Klass and Steffen and published in 2017) have revolutionized the way many *grief professionals* think about grief. For a variety of reasons the more modern, more realistic continuing bonds theory has not yet filtered into the public consciousness on a scale large enough to adequately challenge the still-prevailing stage theories and other linear spinoffs.

One reason is that, unfortunately, most people have never met or spoken to a grief professional; that is, a helping professional who has a sound knowledge base on the subject of grief and has developed comfort and expertise in facilitating the grief process. Another reason continuing bonds theories have not yet become widely known is that these theories are not as neat, tidy, and easy to comprehend as entrenched stage theories. This has led to stubborn resistance to newer ideas and models which cannot be easily summarized and memorized in one sentence, as in, "the stages of grief are ..."

Theorists suspect that for thousands of years many ordinary people with average common sense and wisdom have intuitively believed in and have maintained continuing bonds with their loved ones who have died. I always love it when modern rigorous scientific research discovers and validates something that has been established folk wisdom for millennia.

I believe that in modern times many bereaved people have maintained continuing bonds with their loved ones who have died. However, they are often reluctant to mention their on-going relationships with the deceased for fear of being judged, discounted or scolded. Many have had the experience of hearing reactions from the well-intentioned but uninformed such as, "You have to move on, you can't live in the past, you're being morbid, yada, yada, yada..." at the mere mention of the name of the person who has died.

People who make this kind of comment are often carrying around a huge load of unresolved grief. Consciously or unconsciously they are terrified of their own grief coming to the surface. They don't want to be reminded of your loss lest they be reminded of their own.

So there are many of us who have the intuitive wisdom to maintain continuing bonds, but we keep our on-going relationships with the deceased a secret, even when these bonds are the one thing that is most helpful to us in coping with the loss. Now the bereaved can speak about the continuing bonds and notice the response from others. Note the ones whose eyes light up in recognition and the ones who frown. If they frown or say something to discourage your continuing bonds, you will know not to mention this to them in the future.

...OR depending on the circumstances and the setting when you get that frown you might say (in your own words, of course) that modern scientific research has shown that maintaining our relationships with deceased loved ones is one form of healthy coping. However, *don't* get drawn into a debate or an argument trying to convince someone of this. Simply share the information matter-of-factly.

My former therapist, an extremely wise woman, had a small needlework piece in her office which read, "Never try to teach a pig to sing. It wastes your time and annoys the pig." Remembering this bit of wisdom has served me well many times.

Another reason continuing bonds theory is not yet widely known is that the original 1996 book and its follow-up were both written *by* scholarly scientists presumably *for* scholarly scientists. For evidence of this, go to Amazon.com and read for free the table of contents and the first few pages of these two books. Even with a master's degree and above average reading comprehension skills, this was laborious and intimidating reading for me. I'm pathetically challenged in math but I've always been an above average reader.

I appreciate and applaud the priceless contribution of Klass and his colleagues. However, I would not recommend the two ground-breaking volumes compiled and edited by Klass and others unless the reader enjoys academic or scientific publications.

Fortunately for the rest of us, there are others who have read the books and translated them for those like myself who do not particularly enjoy academic scientific reading. For example, I highly recommend the website https://whatsyourgrief.com. It is an excellent multi-faceted resource and includes several articles about continuing bonds theory.

Specifically, I would recommend both of these articles from the "What's Your Grief?" website:

- "16 Tips for Continuing Bonds with People We've Lost" found at https://tinyurl.com/yxaylm7r
- "A Grief Concept You Should Care About: Continuing Bonds" at https://tinyurl.com/yysqqjos

Also see the article "Five Things You Should Know about

Continuing Bonds" from the website www.thefuneralfriend.com at https://tinyurl.com/yxptlzj8 . Enjoy your explorations into continuing bonds theory, but be sure to come back here – there's much more good stuff to come!

We have devoted an entire chapter to the number one most common and most damaging falsehood about grief (which could just as easily be called falsehoods numbers one through seven). Refuting the remaining nineteen falsehoods, half-truths and flat-out lies will require only one chapter which will lead us into the additional strategies for grief resolution and integration.

If you have read through to this point, you deserve applause and appreciation. Take a deep breath and know that by staying with this difficult subject, you are exhibiting courage, strength, and resilience. Consider yourself applauded and appreciated by Grace Terry!

For Personal Refection, Journaling, and Group Discussion

1. What has been your experience with "the five stages of grief" theory? Have you found it to be helpful or not helpful?
2. Fred Rogers, host of *Mister Rogers' Neighborhood* said, "As different as we are from one another, as unique as each one of us is, we are much more the same than we are different. ..." Your thoughts?
3. His Holiness, the Dalai Lama, said, "When we meet real tragedy in life, we can react in two ways – either by losing hope and falling into self-destructive habits, or by using the challenge to find our inner strength." Your response?
4. "Imagine a spiral as a model of the grief pathway over time. Think of a slinky toy that stretches indefinitely in two directions at a forty-five degree angle. One end extends downward to the earth and the other end stretches upward to the heavens. Each curve of the spiral represents an occasion of expressing and releasing a layer of emotional pain from our hearts and accepting caring energy into the empty space. Every time this happens, the spiral extends one more curve upward or higher and

simultaneously extends one more curve downward or deeper." Your thoughts?

5. "When a re-cycling occurrence is triggered by that song, that scent, that date on the calendar, another loss, a dream, seeing that stranger in a crowd who looks familiar - or by any other stimulus - a deeper layer of grief has been brought to the surface to be expressed and harmlessly released. It's all part of the process of integration..." Do you remember instances of "re-cycling" of grief?

6. Carl Sandburg said, "Life is like an onion. You peel it off one layer at a time, and sometimes you weep." Your thoughts?

7. In your own words, how would you explain continuing bonds theory of grief? Do you think the theory has merit or relevance for you?

CHAPTER 3

NINETEEN TRUTHS TO SET YOU FREE!

I compiled this pervasive *MIS*-information about grief over thirty years of personal experience in my own conscious grief journey and almost forty years of professional experience serving as a companion to others on their journeys. I have included on this list only those falsehoods which I have encountered repeatedly.

I list each erroneous idea and then offer my own personal and professional *opinion* as to the truth. I stress the word "opinion." I have mine and others are free to differ. I am perfectly comfortable with differences of opinion.

Ideas that I consider false may be true in your experience. Things I consider to be true based on my experience may not fit with yours. I do believe that if you continue with your reading you will find something of value. Take what you like and leave the rest.

I heard one time, "The truth will set you free, but first it will p*ss you off!" Some of the truths written here may give great relief, some may bring awareness that at first is painful, and some may absolutely p*ss you off! Whatever your reaction to anything included here, just pause, inhale, exhale, and keep reading.

In some cases, my opinions stated in this chapter will be a brief repetition of information stated in earlier chapters. While I have attempted to minimize restatement, I maintain that some truths are worth repeating. As you read through the remainder of this chapter, make note of any falsehoods and clarifications that you find particularly interesting, relevant to your life, or significant.

FALSEHOOD #1:
Grief refers only to those emotions
people experience when someone dies.

TRUTH: Grief refers to the body/mind/spirit response to the perception of ANY significant loss. The loss may be the death of a significant person or the result of any number of life events, whether the events are in one's own life or in the life of another. Life events that create grief include but are not limited to:

- divorce (one's own divorce or another's divorce if another's divorce directly affects you),
- disability, (one's own or another's if another's directly affects you),
- disease, (one's own or another's....you get it),
- disfigurement,
- miscarriage,
- relocation,
- disillusionment,
- trauma of any kind,
- downsizing/unemployment or other financial reverses,
- estrangement,
- incarceration,
- natural disasters,
- pet loss,
- abuse,
- addiction,
- and others.

I repeat for emphasis, *anything that disrupts a person's sense of normalcy is a grief issue.* As you continue reading keep in mind that with few obvious exceptions, everything written in this book about grief resolution and integration applies to grief resulting from *any loss.*

The loss may be tangible or intangible. For an example of an intangible loss from my own life, one of my most intense grief experiences has been grieving the loss of a childhood that never was possible in my early life. With absolutely no indulgence in blame, self-pity, or victimhood, I can honestly say that for me there were no "carefree childhood days" as I matured from infancy through adolescence into adulthood.

For as far back as I can remember, I felt overly responsible for the well-being of my parents and my siblings. My mother used to say to others about me, "She's been an old woman all her life." I could tell by the way she said it that it was not meant as a compliment. I could also tell that she had no clue whatsoever that she may have contributed in any way to my "oldwomanhood."

As an adult in therapy, I grieved the loss of my childhood. I cried oceans of tears, I raged, and I shook with terror, all in an atmosphere of caring support and safety. I learned the difference between being "responsible for" and being "responsible to." I learned about healthy boundaries. I learned compassion and forgiveness for myself and others. I learned *"it's never too late to have a happy childhood."*

Whether the loss is tangible or intangible, in all cases significant losses trigger intense emotional responses which then trigger physical, cognitive, and spiritual reactions. In truth there is no separation between emotional, physical, cognitive and spiritual health. When any one is impacted, all are impacted.

I'm told that in Asian cultures there is no language or vocabulary to differentiate and separate the emotional, spiritual, social, cognitive and physical dimensions of a person. Reportedly, such compartmentalization is a construct unique to the modern western way of thinking. Grief impacts all dimensions of the person who is grieving, whether it is the result of a death or some other loss.

FALSEHOOD #2:
It is best to avoid, deny, or medicate grief,
rather than to allow its expression and progression.

TRUTH: Denying, avoiding, or medicating grief carries high risk for life-limiting emotional and/or physical illness. Consciously attending to grief has many benefits, including post-traumatic growth. (Further explanation in earlier chapters.)

FALSEHOOD # 3:
The best way to manage grief
is to stay busy.

TRUTH: Staying constantly busy to avoid grief is self-defeating. It is much wiser to plan time for being busy with pleasant activity and also plan time for active, conscious, intentional grief work described in detail in later chapters. Busy-ness is highly overrated in our culture.

FALSEHOOD #4:
Talking about grief only makes it worse.

TRUTH: Talking about grief with a kind, empathetic, patient listener *with the conscious intention of releasing pain* can absolutely save one's life and contribute immensely to the quality of one's life. More about conscious intention to release pain in the next chapter.

FALSEHOOD #5:
Tears are a sign of weakness
and loss of control.

TRUTH: This is one of the most damaging flat-out lies told and believed in modern times. If you have any doubt that this is a flat-out lie, first do an internet search using the search words "the value of tears." You will be directed to an abundance of scholarly sources documenting the health benefits of tears. Even the Bible says,

"(There is) a time to weep and a time to laugh, a time to grieve and a time to dance.... (Ecclesiastes 3:4). This is ancient universal wisdom.

Consider that every healthy human has functioning tear ducts. We would not have evolved as a species with tear ducts if the tear ducts did not serve a useful survival function. When we freely shed tears *without shame and with the conscious intention of releasing pain*, the tears serve a cleansing and restorative purpose. One professional grief support provider I once knew said, "Grief takes time, talk and tears." I concur (with certain caveats I will mention later).

When I was employed as a hospice bereavement counselor making home visits to those who had recently had a loved one die under our care, *every single time* a family member would become tearful while talking with me, they said, "I'm sorry...," Often, the mourner followed the apology immediately with the comment, "I said I wasn't going to do this!" I waited and watched for the first time a bereaved person would *not* apologize for their very appropriate, potentially beneficial tears, but it never came.

My own beloved father, a good person and a good father in many ways, would occasionally use spanking to discipline my siblings and me. Being a very sensitive child, even a mild spanking was devastating to me. When I would cry, my dad would demand, "Dry it up! I'll give you something to cry about!"

Of course, I swallowed my heartbreak and stopped crying. As an adult in therapy, I re-learned to shed healthy tears. I shed buckets of "old tears" that had been withheld for decades. This was a critically important practice for me in getting better.

I once heard, "Tears do for the soul what soap does for the body." I don't remember who said it, but I remembered it because this is true in my experience. Now I do not cry often, but when I do cry I don't apologize for it and I don't shame myself for crying.

If you can shed tears, rejoice! Weeping can be a part of your grief integration process. If you have difficulty allowing yourself to cry, I will offer suggestions in a later chapter that can be helpful.

Remember, you were born with the skill and capacity to release pain through tears. If you have been socialized in a way that makes that near impossible and would like to reclaim this inherent wisdom, in the next section of this book I will help you remember what you knew the day you were born.

FALSEHOOD #6:
Funerals and memorial services are morbid and meaningless
and should be avoided whenever possible.

TRUTH: This is actually half-true. Unfortunately, often funerals and memorial services are missed opportunities to provide real comfort and support to those who mourn as well as to honor a life. This is the reason that so many families today choose not to have any service to mark the end of a life. Another reason is the exorbitant financial costs that can be incurred with funeral and burial expenses.

The good news is *it doesn't have to be this way*. While certain health laws govern disposal of the deceased's remains, the traditional rules of etiquette about funerals/memorial services no longer apply - just as the traditional rules of etiquette about weddings are now considered obsolete.

Today any family can create an occasion that honors the deceased and is appropriate for the family and close friends. This does not have to create a financial hardship for survivors. This assumes, of course, a certain flexibility on the part of the family and on the part of the funeral officiant if there is one.

Some families and officiants are stuck in a cookie cutter "one size fits all" frame of mind. They think there is one right way to conduct an end-of-life service. I would not argue or debate that. I would simply offer the suggestion that there are no laws written that dictate a certain order of service, certain scriptures, or certain music that must be played at every funeral or memorial service. There is plenty of room for individualization.

I also suggest that it is never too late to have a memorial service that is comforting for you. Perhaps you had a loved one who died many years ago and the funeral did not go as you might have wished. You can plan another one if you wish. You can invite friends and family who support you and you can have the kind of memorial service that makes a difference for you. Your author is available to assist if requested. You can contact me through my website www. angelsabide.com.

An excellent resource for planning meaningful funerals and memorial services can be found at the website for Dr. Alan Wolfelt, Founder and Director of the Center for Loss and Life Transition at https://www.centerforloss.com/bookstore/. Dr. Wolfelt is a prolific writer, so if you go to his website use the search function on the site to find books related to funeral planning if that's your primary interest. He has written funeral planning guides for families, for clergy and other helping professionals, and for funeral service providers.

While you are on the Center for Loss website, browse around. Dr. Wolfelt has been very influential in my personal journey and I appreciate, respect, and recommend his work.

Ideally, all families would have some discussion on funeral matters prior to a death. This is where I give my most passionate plea for funeral and burial pre-planning and pre-financing. Beloved reader, if you have never discussed with your family what type of end-of-life care you prefer, please do so right away. Without blame, self-pity, or victimhood, here is my experience which I offer solely as a cautionary tale -

My mother died at age fifty-six in an automobile accident. My father died two years later at age fifty-eight of a heart attack. Neither of them had made any kind of pre-arrangements. They did not have wills. My siblings and I were totally at the mercy of our stepfather and stepmother.

Due to an unusual set of circumstances, I was primarily responsible for planning my mother's funeral on the saddest day of my life. I was left to make dozens of decisions not having any clue as to what might be my mother's wishes.

When my father died, my stepmother arranged an end-of-life service that would have been perfect *for her* if she had been the one being memorialized. The service was in no way reflective of my father and was of no comfort whatsoever to me. In fact, I strongly felt both then and now over thirty years later that the service was an insult to his memory.

Neither Mama nor Daddy left much of a financial legacy. Fortunately, mother's estate was relatively easy to settle although there were disappointments and heartbreaks regarding the disposition of her personal belongings which had little material value but infinite sentimental value. Again, my siblings and I were at the mercy of our stepfather.

However, it took *twenty years* to finally settle the matter of a one-acre parcel of land that my father and step-mother jointly owned when he died. It took twenty years plus attorneys plus periodic unpleasant negotiations to finally reach an agreement concerning the one acre, all based on a matter of principle rather than on the monetary worth of the land.

Also, there were heartbreaks and betrayals related to my father's personal belongings. Several years before he died, when headed into a high-risk but necessary aneurysm surgery, he wrote down a few instructions as to his wishes concerning his few earthly treasures and gave the instructions to our stepmother.

However, he did not place his instructions in a form that was legally binding. He trusted his wife, our stepmother, to carry out his instructions. She allowed my siblings and me to read his instructions, then followed those instructions with which she agreed and ignored those with which she disagreed.

Much of this stress might have been avoided if my beloved parents had made legally binding pre-arrangements for their end-of-life care and for the disposition of their estates including their personal belongings. There are countless similar stories and countless others that are even more disturbing. Imagine if there had been any significant monetary value to my parents' estates! Then things could have become even crazier!

Again, my parents were both in their fifties when they suddenly died. Whatever your age, if you are a legal adult you can decide how you want to have your body treated when you die and how you would want to be memorialized when you die. You can make arrangements for the settlement of your estate. *Do this for yourself, your family, your friends, but do it!*

It is never too early to have discussions and to make plans for the inevitable. If you later change your mind you can change the plans. ...but please do not leave your survivors in the position of being forced under pressure to make dozens of difficult decisions on the saddest day of their lives.... And do not make them vulnerable to the peculiarities or profit motives of others or to the legal system that decides for you posthumously if you neglect to decide in advance.

Please plan some celebration of your life which will give comfort and support to those who will miss you when you have physically exited this life. Once you have made all plans and arrangements, be sure to let your next of kin know where and how to access the information regarding your plans.

If there are those in your life you will miss when they make their transitions, talk to them about their wishes for their own end-of-life care. The more highly resistant you are to this idea, the more you need to face this challenge and master it.

For more specific suggestions on facing this challenge, see my book titled *"Ten Simple Strategies for a Happier You"* (available on amazon.com in paperback and e-book formats), especially the chapter on "Accepting Your Mortality and Your Immortality."

FALSEHOOD #7:
Grieving shows a lack of faith.

TRUE: People with great faith grieve. Grieving does not negate our faith. Grief simply demonstrates that we are human.

It is true that traumatic loss at times challenges our faith. Depending on how we respond to our loss, the grief journey can also be a time when faith is strengthened and renewed. In my own grief journey I have had experiences that challenged my faith and experiences that strengthened and renewed my faith.

The grief journey is inherently a spiritual journey; that is, grief always has spiritual implications and dimensions. Grief activates questions about the nature and meaning of life, about the afterlife, about the nature of the divine and the role of the divine in our lives, and other mysteries. These are vitally important spiritual matters and how we address them can greatly impact the quality of our lives indefinitely, for better or for worse.

Addressing this topic fully would require a separate book-length manuscript in itself. For now, I will simply encourage all readers to take advantage of a wealth of resources available to assist the spiritual seeker.

If you like, you can start with my thoughts about the difference between spirituality and religion and suggestions for celebrating your spirituality in my book titled *"Ten Simple Strategies for a Happier You"* (available on amazon.com in e-book and paperbaack formats). There is an entire chapter on "Celebrating Your Spirituality."

FALSEHOOD #8:
Time heals all wounds.

TRUTH: Time alone heals very few, if any, wounds, especially wounds that are more emotional and spiritual than physical. Here is an example that always comes to my mind. A couple came to me for marriage counseling. They were in their late forties. They had been married young, later divorced, then remarried. Coming to me for marriage counseling was their last stop on the way to divorce court again.

When the two were still very young, their toddler daughter was killed in a tragic accident. As they mentioned the death briefly, it was clear that the pain of that loss was still present with them just as much as on the day of their daughter's death.

Time alone had done nothing to soften their grief. The pain of the death had a huge negative impact on their first marriage and was now having a similar negative impact on their second attempt at creating a functional relationship. Nothing significant had really changed during the years they were divorced. Their grief had not gone away in over twenty years. It had not even faded.

Another remarkable client I knew many years ago was a brilliant, beautiful woman who had advanced in a male-dominated profession to a position of great responsibility, authority and status. In our first session, she kept speaking about "the accident" as if I understood her reference.

After she mentioned this several times, I said, "I'm sorry, I'm not sure what you mean by 'the accident.'" She was shocked that I didn't know she was referring to a disastrous industrial explosion at her workplace years before we met.

When the accident occurred, it was so horrific that it did make the national news briefly but I had heard no mention of it since. Seven people died instantly that day, all of whom were personally known to my client. The force of the blast and the chemicals that caused it were such that there was no identifiable trace remaining of the bodies of my client's seven co-workers.

After the tragedy her employer provided no trauma debriefing or grief support of any kind. My client's work was highly competitive and highly classified. She and all others connected with the company at the time of the explosion were told never to speak of it at work or outside of work. If they did dare to speak of it and this could be proven, they would instantly be terminated and prosecuted. She only spoke of it to me because she knew that federal law protected her confidentiality in my office.

She decided at the time of the tragedy that the deaths were all her fault and that she could have prevented the loss of life "if only..." Such irrational guilt is very common in early acute grief and sometimes gradually dissipates, depending to a great extent on the support that the bereaved person allows and receives. Not being allowed to aknowledge the loss to a single soul, the guilt only became greater for her as years past.

It was if she was frozen in time. All her grief about the fatal accident was just as raw and excrutiating at the time of her first session with me as it had been on the day of the explosion years earlier. When she presented for therapy she was in her early fifties and suffered with physical, emotional, and spiritual health challenges typical of a much older person.

She recited a long litany of names of people who had also been in top management positions at the company at the time of the accident and who had since died suddenly of stress-related causes such as heart attacks. Without intervention, she would surely have died a premature death directly related to the unattended grief from the fatal explosion at her workplace.

As mentioned before, an experienced bereavement counselor I once knew said, "Time, talk, and tears is what it takes." Regrettably, it was so many years ago that I do not remember her full name or I would give her full credit here for her wisdom. Her first name was Patty.

I would add to the "time, talk, and tears" idea that talking to just anyone about our grief is not recommended. We choose carefully to whom we speak about our deepest pain. I will discuss choosing a grief mentor/companion/coach in a later chapter.

FALSEHOOD #9:
The goal of bereavement care is to help the bereaved
get over grief as quickly as possible.

TRUTH: The goal of bereavement care is to provide patient, unconditionally supportive attention, to listen non-judgmentally and empathetically, and to let the bereaved know that they are not alone in their pain. Also, good bereavement care often includes grief education to clarify the care receiver's understanding of the realities of grief.

FALSEHOOD #10:
No one can really help grieving persons with their grief.

TRUTH: This is a flat-out lie. Humans were never intended to grieve alone. We are not equipped to do so. Humans are meant to grieve in supportive community. The modern patriarchal myth of self-sufficency just does not work in matters related to grief and loss. Personally, I don't think it works well anytime in any area of human endeavor, but I'm absolutely sure it doesn't work in matters related to grief and loss. If it did, we would all be healthier and happier. Which is related to...

FALSEHOOD #11:

Only people with advanced specialized formal professional education and a professional license can help grieving persons.

TRUTH: Again, this is a flat-out lie. In fact, there are many excellent professionals with specialized formal education and professional licenses who are not especially good at providing bereavement care. Grief is *not* pathology. It is normal and natural and is typically not addressed in professional training beyond a superficial, outdated "Five Stages of Grief Ending in Acceptance" lecture.

Just as in the example above of the woman who felt responsible for a fatal workplace accident, unattended grief can become complicated grief and can mutate into serious mental health challenges which do require the services of a licensed professional for proper care. I write more about complicated grief in a later chapter.

However, any caring person can be coached and supported so that they can provide excellent bereavement care in most circumstances. They only have to learn the truth about grief and do their own grief work to be qualified. More about this later in the chapter on "Finding Your Grief Companions."

FALSEHOOD #12:

If we talk with someone who has recently experienced
a traumatic loss, it is best to say something like,
"I know just how you feel," or
"God does not give us more than we can bear," or
"You have to move on with your life."

TRUTH: People make these statements because this is the kind of comments they have heard when grieving themselves or they have overheard these comments spoken to other people who are grieving. People who say these things are well-intentioned but lack knowledge and understanding and have had no proper role models. Unfortunately, sometimes comments like this do more harm than good. Please continue reading.

FALSEHOOD #13:

If we see someone who has recently experienced a traumatic
loss, it is best not to mention the loss
because we might upset them.

TRUTH: This is another flat-out lie. Recently bereaved people are ALREADY upset. They often become more upset because everyone they know seems to be awkwardly avoiding the subject of the loss. They feel abandoned and discounted. I have had many, many people tell me this and my heart breaks when I hear it. *It doesn't have to be this way.*

Rather than avoid talking about a loss, or mouthing platitudes to fill up empty silence, a concerned friend or family member might look softly into the eyes of the bereaved and gently say something like, "I care about you. I can't imagine what it's like for you since your loss, but I'm guessing it's hard. Tell me how you're *really* doing. ..." Then stop talking and wait patiently for the answer and breathe, breathe, breathe. ...

If the person truly doesn't want to talk about it, they won't. But if your caring inquiry is sincere, just the invitation to tell the emotional truth is meaningful and appreciated. If they do respond honestly to your inquiry and tell you how they are *really* doing, just breathe, wait, and know that whatever they say can be answered with, "I hear you." It is enough.

Everyone needs to be heard regularly and routinely. People who are grieving need even more to be heard.

If you ask once and the bereaved person changes the subject or otherwise avoids answering, ask again at the next opportunity. Sometimes people need more than one invitation to talk about how they are *really* doing. Don't push, but let the bereaved person know that you care and that you are willing to listen.

Of course, this kind of caring attention is usually only possible if the concerned person has done their own grief work. More soon to come about doing your own grief work for your own benefit and also in order to be helpful to others.

FALSEHOOD #14:
Reading the right books can resolve grief.

TRUTH: Oh, if only it were that simple. Reading books like this one and others can be helpful in the long-term process of resolving and integrating grief, but reading good information alone cannot do it. Taking the home study course in the privacy of your own home can be only minimally effective. To truly integrate grief requires trusting at least one other person with your pain. More about this later.

FALSEHOOD #15:
Once a person accepts a loss, their grief work is done forever.

TRUTH: In a previous chapter, I have described the on-going nature of grief and the recycling process that that is normal in the grief journey. The nature of life on planet Earth is that change and transition and gains and losses are happening constantly all around us and within us with accompanying grief. The skills and knowledge we learn in order to integrate grief can be applied to any and all of the cycles of our lives, which is "done forever" only when we make our transitions from this life to whatever is next.

FALSEHOOD #16:
Those who grieve correctly experience closure quickly
and life goes back to normal.

TRUTH: The fantasy of closure after a traumatic loss is a a flat-out lie.

According to Curtis Rostad, a Certified Funeral Service Practitioner, there is no such thing as closure. Rostad explains why he thinks the concept of closure is mentioned so often in today's culture. "It should come as little surprise that a generation of people brought up with minute rice, instant coffee and microwave ovens would search for quick relief from something we call grief," he says.

There is plentiful literature readily available debunking the myth of closure. You can easily access it by doing an internet search using the search words "closure in the grief process" or similar words. Of all the things I read when I did my search, the following stood out to me. It was written by Bob Livingstone, a Licensed Clinical Social Worker in private practice in San Francisco, California, who observes:

"We are brainwashed by television and movies at a very young age that there is a glorious, happy ending at the end of every story. This phenomenon instructs us that our lives should always include happy endings. We are taught that anything less than total fulfillment and smiles all around amounts to dismal failure. We are taught this concept called closure. It is a term used often in contemporary media and it means to heal a personal loss or trauma such as death of a loved one, being abused by a parent or being a child of an alcoholic parent. After this process, we are supposed to ride off into the sunset with this emotional pain never darkening our door step again.

"Well, this is actually impossible to accomplish unless you get total amnesia. If you have the expectation that you will not have any sad or frightening memories about this trauma once you have believed you have fully healed, you will find yourself deeply disappointed and frustrated.

"*Memories and feelings about the trauma are likely to come up from time to time. Just because the memories continue to arise don't mean that you haven't worked through your issues.* It only means that *as humans, memories and feelings will continue to move in and out of our awareness* unless you are deeply repressing them. ...

"The word closure implies that all of the chaotic feelings and frightened memories get placed in a box with a bright color ribbon tied in a bow. This bow somehow prevents the sense of overwhelm from clouding your sense of well-being.

"*... Real healing is not that tidy and straight forward a process. Authentic healing is different for each individual. Different stages of grief and loss may be wonderful guides for some, but there is no real evidence that these stages actually occur in an explicit order or at all....*" (Italics added)

Does any of this sound familiar? It sounds to me as if Bob is describing what I would call re-cycling. ...and that last sentence is a direct challenge to stage theory ending in acceptance.

FALSEHOOD #17:
Children do not grieve.
They don't understand what is happening.

TRUTH: Children absolutely do grieve. They may not understand what is happening but neither do adults and we know with certainty that adults grieve. Working with children is a specialized expertise that I have never cultivated, but I know this for sure: Many of the adult therapy clients I have known (both men and women) had traumatic losses in childhood which were never properly attended.

Unattended grief in childhood is a setup for a lifetime of unnecessary struggle emotionally, spiritually, socially, and even physically. Remember, there is no true separation between these varied dimensions of the self.

I have previously mentioned Dr. Alan Wolfelt's website and on-line bookstore, www.centerforloss.com/bookstore. There are excellent resources in this on-line bookstore for those concerned about children.

Another excellent resource is the website for The Dougy Center for Grieving Children and Families, https://www.dougy.org/grief-resources/how-to-help-a-grieving-child/. Also, be aware that many hospices have specialized bereavement programs to provide for the care of children who have experienced loss.

You can find an excellent article and resource from the Eluna Network at https://tinyurl.com/y545r3ft. According to the website https://elenanetwork.org.

> *"The mission of Eluna is to support children and families*
> *impacted by grief or addiction. Our innovative resources*
> *and programs address the critical needs of children*
> *experiencing powerful, overwhelming and often*
> *confusing emotions associated with the death of someone*

close to them or substance abuse in their family. No child should have to face these struggles alone, and our unique programs bring kids together to ease their pain and provide the tools to help restore hope."

Do not neglect a child who has suffered a loss, even if the loss seems as simple as a relocation. Our precious children are our hope for future. Caring for them is a sacred trust and a sacred responsibility. Children who grieve need informed, loving attention.

When the grief of children is properly attended, the children acquire knowledge, coping skills and resilience that will serve them well for the rest of their lives. Also, by learning to support children in their grief, you will learn many truths that will be helpful to you and to the child inside of you.

FALSEHOOD #18:
Men do not grieve.

TRUTH: This is a flat-out lie. Men absolutely do grieve and are sometimes criticized or judged because typically they do not grieve the way that women grieve.

I have mentioned the patriarchy repeatedly in earlier chapters. One of the most damaging traits of patriarchal culture is the embedded stereotypes imposed upon men, who are expected to be always "strong" (that is to say, rational, logical, and unemotional), in charge, in control, and self-sufficient. These expectations rob men of their humanity.

Tom Golden, LCSW, is a recognized authority on the subject of men and grief. He teaches that there may be a style of grieving and healing to which men gravitate more readily than women. In his book *Swallowed by a Snake: The Gift of the Masculine Side of Healing*, he observes, "The masculine side of healing is not as accepted a mode of healing as the more traditional verbal and emotional expressions. It tends to be quieter and less visible, less connected with the past and more with the future, [and] less connected with passivity and more aligned with action...."

Gender differences in grief and mourning have been the subject of intense scholarly research in recent years. This is a fascinating subject worthy of much more attention that we can give it here. Once again, I would encourage anyone with a special interest in this topic to do an internet search using the search words "men and grief."

FALSEHOOD #19:
Professionals do not grieve and if they do,
they are being unprofessional.

TRUTH: Professionals are human; therefore, they grieve. No amount of "professionalism" immunizes a person from grief. In this case, professionalism simply means that helping professionals attend to their own grief *outside of their relationships with their client/patients/students/congregants* so that they can more skillfully attend to their clients without being distracted by their own issues.

To any helping professional reading this, including but not limited to medical professionals, mental health professionals, clergy, funeral service professionals, first responders, any who work in the corrections or penal systems, and educators, *your work is sacred work.* In order to do it well and joyfully, you absolutely must be mindful of tending your own soul. I know you know that. Let this serve as a gentle reminder.

Do not be ashamed of your grief. If you are ashamed of yours, you will subtly or not so subtly convey shame to others in your circle of influence who are grieving, including those you are called to serve.

Respected colleague, please do your own grief work for your own sake and so that you can be most effective in helping your clients, patients, congregants and students do their grief work. Cultivate one or more relationships where you receive unconditional support and honest feedback, whether from a mentor, a peer support group, a therapist, or a spiritual director. You will be happier, healthier, and exponentially better as a helper.

Beloved reader, this concludes our exploration and refutation of twenty half-truths, falsehoods, and flat-out lies rampant in modern western industrialized culture. I sincerely hope this has been helpful. Please take what works for you and leave the rest.

Again, my opinion of the truth in these matters is based on my lived experience as a pilgrim on the grief pathway and as a professional companion and guide to others on the journey for almost forty years. Admittedly, I have strong opinions about all of this. Grief education and coaching has become my greatest passion.

This also completes our exploration of the number one foundation strategy for resolving and integrating grief – learning the truth about it. *We must first know the truth about grief in order to resolve it, integrate it, and learn from it.*

Again, I invite you to pause for a moment of self-congratulation and self-appreciation. Know that I appreciate anew your courage, strength, resilience, and wisdom as evidenced by your moving forward on this pathway. *You are an exceptional human being* or you would not have continued this far on the quest.

This leads us now to explore additional strategies for resolving and integrating grief after taking just a few pages to clarify *exactly* what I mean when I use the terms "grief resolution and integration." Again, I stress that with very few obvious exceptions everything in the book applies to grief resulting from any loss, whether the loss is the physical death of a significant person or some other traumatic loss.

For Personal Reflection, Journaling, and Group Discussion

1. Notice the items you marked as being particularly significant or interesting to you. Journal about them as you feel led. Discuss them with others as you feel is most appropriate and helpful to you.
2. "Consider that every healthy human has functioning tear ducts. We would not have evolved as a species with tear ducts if the tear ducts did not serve a useful survival function. When we freely shed tears *without shame and with the conscious intention of releasing pain*, the tears serve a cleansing and restorative purpose...." Your response?

3. How do you feel about making plans for your physical remains when you die? Have you done so? Have you made pre-payment arrangements? Have you made plans for your funeral or memorial service? Have you made those wishes known to others? Have you discussed with your significant their end-of-life wishes?

4. "The grief journey is inherently a spiritual journey; that is, grief always has spiritual implications and dimensions. ..." Your thoughts?

5. "Humans were never intended to grieve alone. We are not equipped to do so. Humans are meant to grieve in supportive community." Your response?

6. "Unattended grief in childhood is a setup for a lifetime of unnecessary struggle emotionally, spiritually, socially, and even physically." Your thoughts?

7. "Professionals are human; therefore, they grieve. No amount of professionalism immunizes a person from grief." Your thoughts?

CHAPTER 4

GRIEF RESOLUTION AND INTEGRATION

What Exactly is Grief Resolution and Integration?

Dear Reader, having read the previous chapters of this book, you have completed the first critically important strategy toward grief resolution and integration – *you have learned the truth about grief.* If you believe what you have read to be true, your knowledge and understanding on this subject is now far beyond that of the average person in western industrialized culture. Of course, with all due respect, the average person is abysmally and painfully ignorant concerning the reality of grief, so being "far above average" simply means that you are no longer abysmally ignorant.

Lest I sound judgmental and/or critical, let me hasten to add that the fact we are a grief-illiterate nation is no one's fault. I do not judge or criticize. I simply report what I observe. We have evolved as individuals and as a culture to a certain point and we continue to evolve. We are all learning together.

Lest I sound arrogant, please believe that I do not think for a moment that I know everything there is to know about grief. Driven by circumstances and a desperate need to understand myself, my family, my life, and the world I inhabit, I chose grief in my early adulthood as a particular focus of study. ...or you might say grief chose me. Either way I was very familiar with grief by the time I was thirty years old and have continued to learn from it continuously since then.

In my mid-sixties now, I know and understand more than ever before. At the same time it's as if I am barely acquainted with the subject of grief and could spend several more lifetimes learning more and more about this universal human experience.

For now, I teach what I have learned in my personal and professional journey hoping to be helpful and hoping to give others the benefit of my experience. It is my way of passing forward the countless acts of kindness that have been generously extended to me.

Before discussing each additional strategy, I want to clarify EXACTLY what I mean and what I do not mean when using the terms "grief resolution" and "grief integration." I have described briefly in previous chapters my thoughts on this but before moving forward I want to be very clear as to my meaning when I use these phrases.

Thoughtful, highly qualified and credential professionals debate which English word most appropriately describes the point in the grief journey when pilgrims are beyond the most intensely painful and difficult times. As a result, they have become relatively peaceful within about their loss *most of the time*.

Our modern English language reflects our culture's stubborn resistance to revising and updating the idea of "five stages of grief ending in acceptance," in spite of massive evidence that this model is inaccurate and misleading at best. We just do not have a good one-word label for that place on the grief pathway where the most challenging terrain is behind us. We need a new word but as yet I have not discovered or invented one.

After wrestling with this dilemma over and over, I have settled on using "grief resolution." As a grief educator, a writer, and a lover of words, I am not one hundred per cent satisfied with using the word "resolution," but I have not been able to determine a better one.

Definitions of the term "resolution" found in assorted dictionaries include the following:

- a solution, accommodation, or settling of a problem, controversy, etc.
- the solution to a problem,

- the act of solving a problem or finding a way
  to improve a difficult situation,
- the act of solving or explaining a problem or puzzle.

I submit that grief resolution is a state of consciousness; that is, grief resolution is

- an attitude,
- a state of mind,
- a perspective, or
- a frame of mind.

As we know, attitudes are rather fluid and can change moment to moment, hour by hour, and day to day.

Grief resolution is a state of consciousness that can shift rapidly and can also be cultivated. With intentional active grief work and practice, the bereaved can reach this level of consciousness and remain in this state of mind most of the time.

When I use the term "grief resolution," I refer to that interval in the grief journey where grief is no longer considered a problem to be solved, something to "get over" like the flu, an enemy to be conquered, an embarrassment or something shameful. When grief is resolved, the bereaved know both in their heads and their hearts that grief is a normal and natural part of life and therefore there is no shame associated with it.

Indeed, when grief is resolved, the bereaved becomes aware that the "grief journey" is in truth the "life journey," because change, losses and gains, and grief are all part of life. Those who have worked through to grief resolution are pretty much okay with that.

They realize that the most painful and difficult times in life make the joyful times much more precious and appreciated. Having reached grief resolution, the one who mourns knows in their heart that grief is the price paid for caring and would make the same decision again to care, knowing the cost.

Grief resolution does *not* mean that the pilgrim on the spiral pathway reaches a point where grief is never again painful. It means the pain of grief is no longer constant, frequent, crippling or excruciating. Triggering and re-cycling of painful emotions directly resulting from traumatic loss becomes less and less frequent, less and less severe, and of shorter and shorter duration.

The one who has successfully resolved their grief rarely, if ever, feels the acute intense pain typical of early grief. Where once the pain was sharp and fierce and enormous, it becomes smaller, gentler and softer.

Grief resolution means that the mourner is no longer afraid of the pain, knowing that it is temporary and manageable. When grief is resolved, the bereaved has no need to avoid, flee from or medicate sadness, anger, fear, or guilt *about anything* when a new layer of these feelings comes to the surface to be released.

They only need to pause, breathe and choose their favorite way to express and release the pain (more on this very soon). With practice, expressing and releasing pain becomes as natural as breathing.

Ernest Hemingway wrote in *A Farewell to Arms*, "The world breaks everyone and afterward many are strong in the broken places. ..." Those who arrive at grief resolution are strong in the broken places. When the bereaved achieve resolution of any loss, they build resilience and develop skills for facing all kinds of life challenges.

When mourners achieve grief resolution, they can provide a caring presence for others who grieve without being flooded with their own feelings. They know that a caring presence is a priceless gift and that usually no words are needed except perhaps, "I hear you." They become clear channels of divine healing and peace.

One of my favorite writers and teachers about grief is Dr. Alan Wolfelt, founder and director of the Center for Loss and Life Transition (www.centerforloss.com). Dr. Wolfelt insists that the only appropriate word to use for this milestone in the grief journey is "reconciliation."

For various reasons I respectfully disagree with him on this one point. You might want to read his thoughts about this at https://tinyurl.com/y4nryvcm. In this article Dr. Wolfelt defines the word "reconciliation" in relation to grief, explains what he means when he uses it in this context, and gives indicators of reaching this site on the grief journey. It is an excellent article and I highly recommend it and all of Dr. Wolfelt's writing to my readers.

Whether we call this state of consciousness acceptance,

reconciliation, or resolution, the most important points are as follows:

1. *The horrific pain of early acute grief does not have to last forever and it doesn't have to be repressed.* While there is no magic wand or formula or roadmap to reach a constant pain-free state in this lifetime, pilgrims on the grief pathway can learn to live joyfully and peacefully *most of the time* if they are willing to do the necessary work described in detail in coming chapters;

2. *Grief resolution is a state of emotional and spiritual maturity that does not happen automatically over time.* Reaching this level of maturity requires conscious and conscientious intention and action – soon to be described in great detail;

3. *Reaching grief resolution happens gradually and slowly* but it does happen if we keep consciously moving toward it. C. S. Lewis, the renowned British writer, professor and lay theologian, wrote the book *A Grief Observed* after the death of his beloved young wife, Joy Davidman, from cancer. In describing his grief symptoms as they lessened, he said, "There was no sudden, striking, and emotional transition. Like the warming of a room or the coming of daylight, when you first notice them they have already been going on for some time."

GRIEF RESOLUTION HAPPENS when there is *grief integration*. According to The Center for Complicated Grief at the Columbia University School of Social Work (www.complicatedgrief. columbia.edu):

"Integrated grief is the lasting form of grief in which loss-related thoughts, feelings and behaviors are integrated into a bereaved person's ongoing functioning; *grief has a place in the person's life without dominating*." (Italics added.)

When I think of grief integration, I imagine multiple photographs of a remnant of woven cloth about eighteen inches square. Each snapshot is a moment in time in a life stricken by traumatic loss.

Imagine the first photograph. Notice the remnant of cloth pictured is woven of light, dark, and neutral threads with a few small blotches of dark stain that are barely noticeable. This piece of cloth represents a particular person's life before traumatic loss. The light, dark, and neutral threads represent normal moderate highs and lows in this life. The few small dark stains represent relatively minor losses, heartbreaks, setbacks or disappointments. This is a rather bland, ordinary piece of cloth.

Now imagine that in the second picture, the same cloth has most of the threads covered by a huge black stain with only a narrow irregular margin around the edges left unblemished. The black stain represents a traumatic loss. This is a representation of this same life immediately after a traumatic loss and illustrates how grief can completely overshadow and define a person's life for a time.

Now imagine the next snapshot captures the cloth with a much smaller area covered by the black stain. The weaving in the background incorporates more black threads than were showing in the first snapshot. However, the black threads in the background are arranged so that they help to create an aesthetically pleasing pattern. This piece of cloth represents the same life *after conscious active grief work* (complete description and suggestions to follow). This is a picture of *partial resolution and integration*.

Actually, there could be an infinite number of photographs illustrating partial resolution and integration with intentional grief work. Over time, the black stain could enlarge and contract over and over as grief is repeatedly triggered and recycled in the normal process of grief resolution and integration. Each time the stain enlarges, less and less time is required before it contracts again.

Now imagine the next snapshot shows the remnant of cloth having no dark stain. Instead, it has become a uniquely beautiful tapestry with dark threads integrated into the weaving in a way that makes the lighter colored and neutral threads more vivid. The whole effect is much more remarkable and more appealing than the image of the first piece of cloth.

You may not be able to tell by looking, but this tapestry is *much stronger* and *more durable by far* than when the remnant was pictured in the first photograph. At the same time, it is *softer*. This is *grief integration.*

Imagine another photograph taken still later of the remnant of cloth with new temporary stains representing later losses that are gradually being integrated or woven into the background. *The tapestry gradually becomes more and more complex and beautiful, more and more durable, softer and softer with on-going interweaving and integration.*

A few dark threads might be used to embroider brief words of wisdom and/or an exquisite design on the foreground or around the border of the tapestry. The possibilities for wise words, background patterns and foreground or border designs are infinite. Each and every tapestry represents an extraordinary lifetime of learning and is unique, precious, and priceless. This is an illustration of on-going grief integration and could also be an illustration of post-traumatic growth.

Dear reader, I hope this description of grief integration is helpful in giving you a vision for where you are headed on the grief journey if you continue on the spiral pathway. In the coming chapters I will give you clear roadmap to get you there.

Are you willing to live an extraordinary life which could be represented by a uniquely gorgeous tapestry with lasting words of wisdom? I have lived long enough to know that this is a true possibility for anyone courageous and committed enough to do the work.

Grief work does require courage, perseverance, and humility. Note that courage is not the absence of fear. Those who have courage may be afraid but keep moving and do what they need to do in spite of the fear. Some call this the hero's or the heroine's journey.

Perseverance means you just keep moving forward. If you stumble and fall down, you get up. If you get tired, you pause briefly, gather your strength, and keep moving. Humility means being teachable and willing to follow suggestions.

If you have continued on your grief journey by simply reading this far into this book, you have demonstrated courage, perseverance, and humility. Without all three of these you could not have made it this far. *Grief ain't for sissies!* Congratulate yourself on your success at making it this far.

Inhale, exhale and keep moving. Remember, you do not have to do the work alone. In addition to myself, there are other caring companions for the journey and I will tell you how to find them in a coming chapter. You can do this work. I will walk with you and others will walk alongside you as well. We will cheer you on.

For Personal Reflection, Journaling, and Group Discussion

1. "…the average person is abysmally and painfully ignorant concerning the reality of grief…" Would you agree or disagree? Please explain your answer.

2. In your own words, describe the state of consciousness (attitude or state of mind) called grief resolution.

3. Ernest Hemingway wrote, "The world breaks everyone and afterward many are strong in the broken places. …" How does this apply to grief?

4. *"Are you willing to live an extraordinary life which could be represented by a uniquely gorgeous tapestry with lasting words of wisdom?* I have lived long enough to know that this is a true possibility for anyone courageous and committed enough to do the work." Your response? If your grief journey resulted in your being able to share brief words of wisdom with others, what would you want those words of wisdom to be?

5. "If you have continued on your grief journey by simply reading this far into this book, you have demonstrated courage, perseverance, and humility. …" Your reaction?

PART II
MORE STRATEGIES

CHAPTER 5

SET YOUR INTENTION

Now that you know the truth about grief (grief resolution strategy number one) and know exactly what I mean when I use the phrases "grief resolution" and "grief integration," we are ready to discuss *additional* strategies for living well after traumatic loss.

This chapter is to emphasize that in order to reach the level of consciousness I call grief resolution, it's important for you to consciously commit yourself and decide clearly that you are willing to express and release the pain of your grief. We call this decision-making process *setting your intention for grief resolution.*

Dr. Wayne Dyer was an internationally renowned author and speaker in the field of self-improvement. Interestingly, his website states, "In 2015, he left his body, returning to Infinite Source to embark on his next adventure." He wrote more than 40 books during his lifetime, including *The Power of Intention: Learning to Co-create Your World Your Way,* published in 2010.

Dr. Dyer defined intention as "a strong purpose or aim, accompanied by a determination to produce a desired result..." He added, "Our intention creates our reality."

I has found the process of clearly setting my intention to be incredibly powerful in reaching my most challenging goals. Setting an intention is a life-changing practice you can use in any area of your life where you hope to achieve greater results. It works.

I have been inspired for many years by the following, written in 1951 by the mountaineer William Hutchison Murray and published in his work "*The Scottish Himalayan Expedition.*" This quote does not specifically use the word "intention," but what he describes as "the moment one definitely commits oneself" sounds to me like another way to say "the moment one sets an intention."

Murray wrote the following compelling passage (italics added) and finished it with two lines he mistakenly attributed to Johann Wolfgang von Goethe. In fact, the concluding couplet was written by Irish poet John Anster.

"Until one is committed there is hesitancy, the chance to draw back, always ineffectiveness. Concerning all acts of initiative and creation, there is one elementary truth, the ignorance of which kills countless ideas and splendid plans: *that the moment one definitely commits oneself, then Providence moves too. All sorts of things occur to help one that would never otherwise have occurred. A whole stream of events issues from the decision, raising in one's favour all manner of unforeseen incidents and meetings and material assistance, which no man could have dreamt would have come his way.* I have learned a deep respect for one of Goethe's couplets:

> *Whatever you can do, or dream you can do, begin it.*
> *Boldness has genius, power, and magic in it."*

Murray articulated eloquently what I believe is a universal spiritual truth – that *when we humans commit ourselves wholeheartedly to a worthy endeavor (that is, when we set our intention), the whole Universe responds with infinite unconditional support.* I have experienced this miraculous process repeatedly in my own life and I believe it will work for anyone who tests it.

Are you willing to set your intention for grief resolution and receive "a whole stream of events issuing from that decision, raising in your favour all manner of unforeseen incidents and meetings and material assistance which you could not have dreamt would come your way?" What do you have to lose except your misery?

Some readers may think that this strategy is a given and mentioning it is an unnecessary waste of words. However, in my thirty plus years of providing grief companionship and mentoring, I have known numerous mourners who insisted on clinging tightly to their pain. Without criticism or judgment, I have observed that for a variety of reasons some bereaved persons are unwilling to allow themselves any relief from suffering.

Some feel so guilty they think they deserve to suffer for the rest of their lives. Others are extremely angry and think that by releasing their anger they condone actions they feel are unforgivable. Still others seem to think that if they stop feeling so horribly sad, this would be some sort of betrayal of the person who had died or a relationship that had ended. Some are so afraid of their grief and of the unknown future created by their loss they are emotionally paralyzed. In some cases, nothing would persuade the grieving person to consider other possibilities.

I have known others who were very attached to their role of "helpless victim," typically adopted long before the traumatic loss in their lives. When people adapt the identity of "helpless victim" early in their lives, experiencing traumatic loss only contributes to the persona. Sometimes they refuse to give up their victimhood in order to develop a more life-enhancing practice of self-responsibility.

Your author is intimately acquainted with this dynamic. I was in therapy for years before re-deciding definitively that I am *not* a victim.

Sometimes the bereaved person becomes so identified with and defined by their grief that they cannot imagine themselves without it. I have actually had people say to me, "Without my grief, I don't know who I will be..."

You might wonder, if people are so resistant to releasing the pain of grief why would they see a grief therapist? Surely you have heard the adage "misery loves company." Some people seem to want a grief coach or therapist to give them sympathy and keep them company while they hold onto their pain.

These people also want to be able to say, "I went to see a grief therapist and it didn't help...My case is so unique/extreme/severe that no one can help me. ...but sit for a while and give me some attention and sympathy anyway." Saying "I went to see a grief therapist and it didn't help" is much more powerful than saying, for instance, "I've read lots of books about grief and none of them helped."

Again, I offer these observations without judgment or criticism. I'm not here to say that these reasons for resistance are bad or wrong. I'm saying that various factors hinder some people from moving forward on the spiral pathway of grief to reach grief resolution and integration. Thankfully, these are the exceptions rather than the rule. Thankfully, many of these exceptions decide to release their attachment to their pain once they know the truth about grief as discussed in previous chapters.

So, dear reader, please stop now and locate your journal and a pen or pencil. I will wait. Please do this.

Now, take a deep breath, let it out, and ask yourself the following questions.

Am I determined to do whatever it takes to find a way to release my pain and eventually reach that level of consciousness called grief resolution?

Am I ready and willing to set my intention for grief resolution so that I can live happily and peacefully most of the time in spite of my losses. ...

Notice the first thing that comes to your mind after asking yourself these questions, write it down, then keep writing until you feel complete. Don't worry about grammar, penmanship, punctuation or spelling. Just keep writing and get your thoughts down on paper. It's important. Whatever it is, write it down.

If your answer was an enthusiastic "YES," – great! In this case, I highly recommend you do the writing exercise just below to crystalize your intention.

If your answer was "no" or "maybe, but..." or "yes, but..." *and you would like to get to a definitive and enthusiastic "YES,"* consider the following:

Matt Valentine writes weekly on his blog, Buddhaimonia.com, about everything from spirituality to self-mastery. In an article titled *"How to Harness the Power of Intention and Use It to Your Advantage,"* (found at https://tinyurl.com/y5sae5qx), he writes:

"The power of intention ... is a continuous, consistent use of the mind in a focused manner... there are three steps necessary to fully utilize the power of intention:

1. Decide what you want: By definition, to use the power of intention, you need to know what you're aiming for. If you don't know this, you'll never be able to utilize this power effectively.

2. Get clear on your why: Why do you want what you want? ... Getting clear on your *why* gives power to your intention.

3. Visualize: Knowing what you want and why you want it serves as a foundation, and visualization is the future-planning version of intention-based exercises. It shows you where you're going and helps you map out a path to get there."

So, dear one, *if you want to be clearer and more definite in setting your intention for grief resolution and/or if you want to get to a clear and definitive "YES,"* take Matt Valentine's three steps as follows:

FIRST, *if you're sure you want to reach grief resolution* as described earlier in this book, in Step One write down in your own words exactly what you want. Write down a detailed description of exactly what grief resolution means for you. There are no wrong answers.

SECOND, write down exactly *WHY* you want to reach grief resolution. Be as honest, specific, and detailed as possible. Dig deeply until you find the whole truth. There are no wrong answers.

THIRD, inhale slowly, exhale slowly, take another slow deep breath, then close your eyes and visualize yourself having reached grief resolution. Give yourself plenty of time. Don't rush it. Allow it. Continue to breathe slowly and deeply.

In your visualization, notice the expression on your face. Notice the details of your appearance. Notice what you are wearing and what you are doing and with whom. Notice any sounds or smells or feelings (your own feelings or the feelings of others in the image). Stay with that imagery until you feel complete for now, then open your eyes and

...breathe, breathe,

B R E A T H E.

Now ask yourself the following questions again, and answer as honestly as possible,

Am I determined to do whatever it takes to find a way to release my pain and eventually reach that level of consciousness called grief resolution?

Am I ready and willing to set my intention for grief resolution so that I can live happily and peacefully most of the time in spite of my losses?

If your answer this time was anything other than a clear and definite "YES!" I encourage you to do either or both of the following: 1) talk this over with someone you know and trust, and/or 2) go to my website (www.angelsabide.com) and schedule a FREE 30-minute one-to-one coaching session as soon as possible. Perhaps I can assist you in setting that clear, unqualified intention.

Do one or both of these things if you *really* want to reach grief resolution with all its benefits. *Don't* do either of these if you would rather stay stuck indefinitely in the painful quagmire of grief to collect benefits there. You may prefer the benefits of staying stuck to the benefits of moving forward. If you would rather stay stuck, I sincerely respect your choice to do so. When you are ready to come out of the muck, you can contact me or someone else who can give you a hand up and out. In the meantime, keep reading.

If you have reached the "YES" answer to setting your intention for grief resolution, write down the following:

"I now set my intention to do whatever is necessary to release the pain of grief and reach the state of consciousness known as grief resolution. I stay focused on this intention and devote the necessary time, energy, and effort to achieving this purpose, knowing that the results are well worth the investment."

Sign and date this statement. Share it with at least one other person, someone you trust to accept and support you even if they don't completely understand it. Do these things *only if you want to reach grief resolution.*

If for any reason you're not sure that you want to resolve your grief, write the statement above but don't sign it right now. Perhaps you will be ready to set your intention on a later date. You can take all the time you need. Just remember that *"not to decide is to decide."*

Taking this step can be scary. Remember, courage is feeling the fear and doing what needs to be done anyway. Also remember that you don't have to do grief work alone and you don't have to do it perfectly. You get as many "do-overs" as you need. You won't get a letter grade on this and you won't get expelled from this classroom. We're all here just learning together.

This entire chapter might seem unnecessary to some readers. However, I know how powerful intention is in my own life. I also know that many of us spiritual beings on a human journey consciously or unconsciously sabotage our own happiness, serenity and success. *Those who are grieving in a culture that does not support grief are especially vulnerable to self-sabotage.*

The material in this chapter can't hurt anyone and may make a huge difference for some readers. Sometimes just bringing the self-defeating fears and beliefs into conscious awareness can neutralize their power.

Again, I include this material without any judgment or criticism. I am intimately acquainted with self-sabotage. By young adulthood I had elevated it to a fine art. I'm grateful to all people and circumstances that assisted me in learning better life skills.

Now that we have discussed setting our intention, we can move forward to learn additional strategies for the process of grief resolution and integration. Gentle reader, I encourage you to continue your reading whether or not you have set a clear intention to reach grief resolution. You can revisit this chapter as often as you wish.

We have made tremendous progress together so far. We have learned the truth about grief, debunking a plethora of falsehoods, half-truths, and flat-out lies widely taught and widely believed in our culture. In doing so we learned about continuing bonds, a powerfully enlightening concept.

We have clarified the meaning of the terms "grief resolution" and "grief integration." We have discussed setting our intention for grief resolution.

In our next chapter we will discuss the strategy of finding our soul companions on the grief pathway, particularly finding grief support groups and/or a grief coach/cheerleader/companion/mentor/therapist/ guide.

For Personal Reflection, Journaling, and Group Discussion

1. What is your overall reaction to this chapter?
2. Are there other areas of your life where setting your intention might be helpful?

CHAPTER 6

FIND YOUR GRIEF COMPANIONS

"There are some people who could hear you speak a thousand words and still not understand you. And there are others who will understand without you even speaking a word." – Yasmin Mogahed

Please do not skip this chapter. It may be one of the most important in this book.

In previous chapters I have written more than once, "take what you like and leave the rest." I stand by that.

However, *if you really want to reach grief resolution and integration,* I cannot stress too much how important it is to find at least one and ideally multiple companions for your grief journey. If you are not sure that grief resolution is what you want and/or if you wish to delay reaching grief resolution and integration, a great way to delay indefinitely is to attempt to reach grief resolution alone. Do keep in mind that reaching this state of consciousness takes time and effort in the best of circumstances, so there is really no need to fear getting there too quickly.

Of course, it's entirely your choice as to whether or not you are willing to seek and find this companionship. For whatever it may be worth, understand that *I don't believe it is possible to reach true resolution and integration of grief in emotional isolation.*

Helen Keller is one of my all-time favorite she-roes. For readers who are unfamiliar with her story, Helen was born in 1880 to a well-to-do family in Tuscumbia, Alabama. At nineteen months of age she became ill with a fever that left her both deaf and blind and therefore unable to learn speech.

She was allowed to grow into a completely undisciplined, disabled feral child until her mother found Anne Sullivan to be Helen's teacher. With the assistance of Anne Sullivan and others, Helen Keller learned to communicate and became an internationally known author, political activist, humanitarian and lecturer. She wrote the following:

"You belong to the largest company in the world, the company of those who have known suffering. When it seems that your sorrow is too great to be borne, think of the great family of the heavy-hearted into which your grief has given you entrance and, inevitably, you will feel about you their arms, their sympathy, their understanding."

For the deep soul work of grief, we need to know we are not alone. We need one or more patient, empathetic witnesses who will serve as a quiet, caring presence as we trudge the spiral pathway. We need those who will listen to our grief stories as many times as we need to tell the story. Most of us need to tell it over and over for a time.

When we express and release our pain, we need someone who will immediately direct positive energy toward our hearts to fill up the empty space that was opened up when we released the pain. Receiving the caring energy to fill up the empty space completes one curve of the spiral pathway of grief. The curve is not complete until the empty space is filled with love.

For best results, I recommend a combination of individual and group support. Ideally, you will find one person to provide you with individual support and serve as your primary grief mentor/coach/guide. I use these terms interchangeably. I prefer the term "mentor" but some people are not as familiar with that term as with the term "coach" or "guide."

So now let's discuss where you might find the appropriate companions for this pilgrimage. The quickest, most obvious resource is, of course, Grace Terry.

The following offers are available at the time of this writing. You can go to my website (www.angelsabide.com) and schedule a FREE half-hour get acquainted session. If you and I seem to be a good match for further collaboration, I'll tell you the details about the on-line grief support groups that I offer in exchange for a free-will donation. If you want to schedule additional one-to-one sessions on-line or by phone, I can provide those for a moderate cost.

If you are looking for one-to-one support and would prefer to see someone other than your author, you have various options. Your primary family physician may be able to recommend good sources of bereavement support in your community.

Seeing a professional therapist in your local area would be one option, but I would be sure to find a therapist who has specialized expertise in grief resolution. Otherwise you could end up with someone who only knows "there are five stages of grief ending in acceptance." Seeing a professional therapist can be expensive, but if finances are not a concern this is certainly worth consideration.

Some clergy are trained and available to provide grief support, but these are the exception rather than the rule. Very large houses of worship sometimes have a staff person whose primary responsibility is to provide pastoral care including grief support. Some of these provide excellent bereavement care.

Another source of one-to-one companionship for those who are comfortable with receiving support in a Christian context is Stephen Ministries. Quoting from the website www. stephenministers.org,

"Stephen Ministers are lay congregation members trained to provide one-to-one Christ-centered care. They have a compassionate heart for those who are hurting, and they've been equipped with caring ministry skills by their congregation's Stephen Leaders. A Stephen Minister typically has one care receiver at a time and meets with that person once a week to listen, care, pray, encourage, and offer emotional and spiritual support."

To find a church in your area with Stephen Ministers, do an internet search using the search term "Stephen Ministries in (your state or regional geographic area)." If calling to request a Stephen Minister, be sure to make it clear that you are looking for a grief companion. All Stephen ministers receive intensive training and supervision, but some are much more skilled and comfortable providing grief companionship than others.

Receiving care from a Stephen Minister is usually offered at no cost. Unless you are a contributing member of the church sponsoring the service, I recommend that you send financial donations to the church as you are able in gratitude for the care received. Even small donations are better than no donation. You will receive more if you give something in return.

If you locate someone you consider to be a good candidate to provide you with individual support and act as your primary grief mentor, ask if you can schedule a brief (twenty-thirty minute) complimentary "get acquainted" session with that person. If you are able to get that session scheduled, go with an open mind and chat with the person. Look for authenticity, gentle strength, and good eye contact. Check your gut reaction. While interviewing the candidate, breathe, breathe, breathe...

Here are some questions you might pose to a person you are considering to be your one-to-one grief coach:

- Do you have a personal philosophy of grief care?
- What do you think of the stage theories?
- Are you familiar with Continuing Bonds theory? If so, what is your opinion of it?
- How have you coped with your own losses and grief?
- What kinds of things do you do to take care of yourself?
- If you had it to do over, would you choose the same line of work?
- Have you read the book "The Spiral Pathway of Grief," by Grace Terry? What did you think of it, or (if they haven't read it), it's available on amazon.com.

You may want to interview several people before you make a decision. Trust your intuition in choosing your primary one-to-one grief guide. You don't have to decide on the spot by the end of the get acquainted session if the person with whom you are speaking is the one. You can take your time and think about it.

If you begin working with a particular coach and after a reasonable trial period you are not satisfied with the way things are going, you can choose a different coach. However, I would encourage you to stay with the person long enough to get a true reading of their suitability. Also, be sure to respectfully give the coach honest feedback and be clear with them about what you need and want.

Most pilgrims on the grief pathway get the best results with a combination of individual and group support. Your primary one-to-one grief coach may or may not be the facilitator of your support group. If you are attending weekly support groups, you will not need individual sessions nearly so often.

Whether you attend my grief support groups or groups organized and sponsored by someone else, I highly recommend you seek group support. The quality and quantity of support provided by a well-functioning group is multiplied exponentially beyond what you can receive with individual work alone. Not only are there more people to support you, but there is a synergy created when people gather around a common goal or purpose.

Rigorous scientific research has documented the positive power of peer support for the bereaved. Again, I love it when scientists validate what everyday people with average common sense have known for thousands of years.

See, for example, the article "Peer Support Services for Bereaved Survivors: A Systematic Review," by Paul T. Bartone and others, published in 2017. This article is available to you at https://tinyurl.com/y674yozs . The abstract of the article reads in part (with italics added):

> "This systematic literature review assesses the evidence regarding benefits of peer support services for bereaved survivors of sudden or unexpected death. Reports were included that addressed peer support services for adults who experienced death of a family member, close friend, or coworker. Of the 32 studies meeting all inclusion criteria, most showed evidence that *peer support was helpful to bereaved survivors, reducing grief symptoms and increasing well-being and personal growth.* Studies also showed *benefits to providers of peer support, including increased personal growth and positive meaning in life.* Several studies addressed

the growing trend of Internet-based peer support programs, finding that these are beneficial in part due to their easy accessibility. Peer support appears to be especially valuable for survivors of suicide loss, a result that may be related to stigma and lack of support from family and friends experienced by many suicide survivors. The reviewed studies provide consistent evidence that peer support is beneficial to bereaved survivors."

With the clinical literature documenting that peer support groups are helpful to bereaved survivors of sudden or unexpected death of a family member, close friend, or coworker, especially survivors of suicide loss, we can be sure that groups are helpful to others who are grieving. For more research on the value of group support for the bereaved, do an internet search using the words "effectiveness of bereavement support groups."

The ideal grief support group will most likely include people grieving very recent losses and some who are farther along on the spiral pathway. Your companions may include those who have reached a degree of partial grief resolution and integration. They have waded through the deepest muck and mire of bereavement and have landed on more solid ground. Keep in mind that those who started the active grief journey ahead of you are still subject to intense "re-cycling episodes" so they need your presence as much as you need theirs.

Most hospice care providers offer grief support services at no charge to the community. These services are primarily for survivors who have recently had family members receive end-of-life medical care from the hospice. These same bereavement services are typically available to others from the community on request. Some hospices will provide services to community members who have experienced grief from losses other than from death and some will not.

Calling all the hospice care providers in your area and asking for information about the availability of their bereavement services is a good place to start. Sometimes this information is available on-line but websites tend to provide only the most general information with few details. Call and ask to be added to a distribution list to be notified of upcoming bereavement workshops, groups, retreats, and/or special community memorial services.

Here's something important about bereavement services offered by hospices. To be accredited to receive Medicare reimbursement for medical services, hospice organizations MUST provide bereavement care not only to the families of their patients but also must offer care at no cost to the community. Virtually all hospice care providers need and want that reimbursement to stay in business.

However, bereavement care is *not* a "reimbursable service." To be clear, the hospice organization does not get paid by Medicare or anyone else to provide bereavement care. The cost of providing bereavement care must be absorbed by the organization. This is true whether the hospice is for profit or non-profit. Of course, the management of every hospice provider by necessity is very concerned about the bottom line whether the provider is a non-profit or a for profit organization.

At the same time, Medicare regulations for bereavement care are very vague and non-specific. The National Hospice and Palliative Care Organization (NHPCO) publishes suggested bereavement guidelines and best practices for their members, but even these guidelines are very flexible and vague and acknowledge that different hospices will vary widely in the range and depth of bereavement services offered.

Different hospice organizations have varying philosophies and structures for bereavement care. Be prepared for a wide array of answers and attitudes when you inquire about available bereavement services provided at no cost by hospice care providers in your local area. Some have a strong clear commitment to providing high quality comprehensive bereavement services to their families and to the community. Hopefully you will find this to be true in your local area.

Some larger hospices employ degreed and licensed professionals whose only responsibility is providing bereavement care to the families of deceased patients. Some add bereavement care to the list of responsibilities of those hired primarily to provide other services, such as social workers or chaplains. Some hospices use trained volunteers to deliver bereavement care. Whether bereavement care from hospice is provided by designated staff who only do bereavement care, by staff who do bereavement care as "other duties as assigned," or by volunteers, typically people who provide the care have a genuine interest and an aptitude for the work.

Some hospice organizations offer individual and family grief therapy sessions along with group sessions. Some do not provide individual sessions beyond an initial assessment.

Group sessions offered by hospices are often very structured with a lecture/discussion format and are time-limited. Groups may last for six, ten, or twelve weeks. Such groups may be offered quarterly or only once or twice each year. Be prepared for the possibility that if services are available, it could be months before a new group starts.

You may be fortunate enough to find great support available at no cost through your local hospice. When you call to get information about available services, ask the person with whom you talk for other resources provided in the community as well as services provided by that hospice.

What you locate and attend a grief support group, go with an open mind and a positive attitude. If you go looking for something to criticize, you will find it. If you go looking for the positive aspects of the experience, you will find that. Go to at least three group meetings before deciding whether or not attending the group is worthwhile.

If you can find anything positive to honestly say to the group facilitator, please do so. Overlook any perceived inadequacies unless there is blatant unethical or incompetent behavior (which is highly unlikely). Let them know you appreciate them.

As each person participates in the group, avoid comparing your grief to theirs. Everyone's pain is legitimate. No one's pain can really be measured. Know that by being present and listening you are contributing. When you are ready, be willing to talk.

Expect that you will relate more easily to some group members than to others. Consider that those group members you find to be most annoying could be your most powerful teachers if you ask yourself honestly, "What does it say about me that this person gets on my last nerve?"

When I facilitate a group, I always discuss with the members certain guidelines which are important for a healthy group. These would include:

- Starting and ending on time,
- Agree to disagree without being disagreeable,
- Confidentiality,
- Honesty with love,
- Self-responsibility.

Of these, I might say that a spoken agreement for confidentiality might be the most important. If the commitment to maintain confidentiality is NOT discussed at the beginning of the meeting, consider raising the issue for discussion. Everyone deserves to know that "what is said here stays here."

If you are recently widowed, don't go to the grief support group looking for a new romance. I have known people who did this. This is doomed for failure. Friendship, yes. Romance, no.

Platonic friendships started in the group can be healthy and helpful but go slowly and use caution. Sometimes a group of three or more may decide to go for coffee or a meal after the meeting which can be a better option than going in pairs. If there is a "meeting after the meeting", avoid gossiping about any group members who are not in attendance. Gossip is speaking about someone in a way that you would not want them to overhear.

The quality and quantity of support you can receive in a healthy group is incomparable. However, what you *don't* get in a healthy group is an hour of individual attention with an audience. That is not how healthy groups work. If you feel the need for an hour of undivided attention, schedule an hour of one-to-one time with your primary grief mentor.

Keeping these suggestions in mind will help you get the most benefit from a grief support group. So what do you have to lose, except your isolation and loneliness? Give it a fair try.

If you are comfortable receiving group support that is provided in the context of evangelical Christianity and your grief is directly related to the death of a family member or close friend, consider Griefshare (https://www.griefshare.org). If your grief is directly related to a divorce and you are comfortable with evangelical Christianity, check out Divorcecare (https://www.divorcecare.org).

For those grieving the death of a child of any age for any cause, The Compassionate Friends (compassionatefriends.org) has been providing support to bereaved families for four decades. TCF has a network of over 600 chapters with locations in all fifty states as well as Washington, D.C., Puerto Rico, and Guam.

For those who are grieving a death by suicide, the websites for The Alliance of Hope (https://allianceofhope.org) and The American Foundation for Suicide Prevention (https://afsp.org) can help you find support.

For those grieving losses from causes other than the death of a significant person in your life, do an internet search for specialized information and services. If you cannot find exactly what you are looking for, consider starting your own group. You can use this book as your discussion guide.

Hospitals and larger houses of worship often offer grief support services. Any organization that targets seniors as their primary clientele will often have information about grief support services available in the community. The best funeral service providers will be able to give you information about bereavement care in the community.

Ask around. Call around. Do internet searches using the search terms "bereavement care in (your city or county or state)". Go to websites. If you phone and can actually get a real live person to speak to you, ask not only about bereavement services provided at their setting but also ask if they know about other bereavement service providers in the community.

As a last resort, tell everyone you know that you are starting a book discussion using the book *"The Spiral Pathway of Grief,"* by Grace Terry. If you can attract even one or two other persons to read this book with you and meet regularly either face-to-face, on-line, or on the phone to discuss it, you will find this to be very beneficial and worthwhile.

If you think there is *no way* you would ever start your own group, please consider the following from the website www.copefoundation.org (italics added):

"In 1996, ...Lillian Julien gathered a group of parents living with the loss of a child together for solace and support. They began meeting informally in the safety of each other's homes, *finding comfort and support by being together and freely expressing their grief with people who could understand.* Through this sense of community, they were able to thrive and impact each other's lives *while remaining eternally connected to their children.* They began reaching out to other parents living with the loss of their children, and their group grew into a larger network.

Their experiences together have generated love and hope, resulting in the creation of COPE, a foundation dedicated to providing emotional support to individuals and families who are struggling to cope with life after loss.

COPE was recognized as a 501(c) (3) organization in 1999 and has grown from a small group of families meeting in each others' homes to a support network of over 1000 families meeting, gathering and healing at our new location, COPE at Cedarmere, 225 Bryant Avenue, Roslyn, NY 11576, as well as in generously donated space on Long Island.

COPE's programs have expanded to offer support to all family members including Camp Erin NYC – a free weekend bereavement camp for children and teens ages 6-17 who are grieving the death of someone close to them as well as our Teen General Loss Bereavement Group.

Our monthly healing workshops offer yoga, meditation, Reiki, art, movement, music, breath work and more.

COPE offers special events and workshops, professional forums, a grief support line and an extensive website, ongoing support group meetings and the one-on-one support of peer mentors."

This one woman transformed the pain of her own bereavement into an organization that has made a positive difference for countless individuals and families.

Still struggling to find your peeps?? Go back to the previous chapter and read the quote by William Hutchison Murray. If you have clearly set your intention to do whatever it takes to reach grief resolution and integration, you will attract your ideal grief companions quickly and with relatively little effort. If you are not yet clear with your intention, you will be likely to have more difficulty connecting with your grief mentor and peer companions.

If you have made reasonable good faith efforts and have not found your grief companions, go back to the writing exercise in the previous chapter and do the three steps for the intention "I am willing to receive the benefits of mentoring and peer companionship on the pathway of grief. I intend to do whatever is necessary to attract my ideal grief companions. I am focused on this intention and now devote the necessary time, energy, and effort to achieving this purpose."

Repeat the steps in the previous chapter for this intention. Write it down, date it, sign it, share it with at least one other person, and renew your efforts at reaching out. If finding an individual mentor plus a peer support group seems like too much, do one or the other to start. You will be glad you did. Trust me on this.

Again, I applaud, congratulate and support you one hundred per cent without condition. Finding your "peeps" is a HUGE step in the process of grief resolution and grief integration.

Please consider me one of your peeps. You can send me a message through my website if you wish, even if you do not want to schedule a session with me. Even if we never have direct contact, if you have read this far into my book there is an invisible bond between us that is eternal.

Now inhale, exhale, repeat, and continue to the next chapter. Here we will discuss a multitude of ways you can express and release your grief harmlessly so that you don't carry it in your body, mind, and soul for the rest of your life.

For Personal Reflection, Journaling, and Group Discussion

1. *"There are some people who could hear you speak a thousand words and still not understand you. And there are others who*

will understand without you even speaking a word." (Yasmin Mogahed). Your thoughts?

2. "For the deep soul work of grief, we need to know we are not alone. We need one or more patient, empathetic witnesses who will serve as a quiet, caring presence as we trudge the spiral pathway. We need those who will listen to our grief stories as many times as we need to tell the story. ..." Your reaction?

3. What is your plan for finding your grief companions?

CHAPTER 7

EXPRESS AND RELEASE
PAINFUL FEELINGS

We have reached what may be the most exciting and fundamental information contained in this book. Having set our intention to resolve and integrate our grief and having found our companions, we are now ready to consider the practice of expressing and releasing painful emotions.

This idea of expressing and releasing emotions conveyed in one word is *catharsis* and is as old as the ancient Greeks. According to the webpage https://www.verywellmind.com/what-is-catharsis-

"A catharsis is an emotional release. ...The term itself comes from the Greek *katharsis* meaning 'purification' or 'cleansing.' The term is used in therapy as well as in literature. The hero of a novel might experience an emotional catharsis that leads to some sort of restoration or renewal. The purpose of catharsis is to bring about some form of positive change in the individual's life."

We are simply talking about "letting it out" or what is sometimes called "pouring our hearts out."

There is nothing mysterious or obscure about catharsis. When we become aware of painful emotions, we simply do whatever is most expedient to move that energy through our bodies then expel it through our breath, tear ducts, sweat glands, or pores of our skin or by moving our limbs.

In previous chapters I have mentioned that new-born babies are skilled at expressing and releasing discomfort. I remind you of that now. Spiritual beings on a human journey were *not* created to deny/hide/suppress feelings indefinitely, but were *always* intended to have, express and release emotional responses to life.

This is not rocket science. It's not brain surgery, although it might be considered heart surgery. Thankfully, this kind of heart surgery is performed without incisions.

Admittedly, there are times when for a number of reasons the full expression and release of intense emotions needs to be delayed temporarily but not indefinitely. As we have discussed before, long-term denial and suppression of otherwise healthy and appropriate emotions can eventually result in serious and even life-limiting physical, emotional, and spiritual complications.

I am firmly convinced that the average person in western industrialized patriarchal culture has a mild to moderate to malignant case of "emotional constipation" which began in childhood. Most of us are emotionally impacted with old anger, fear, sadness, guilt and shame. Since some of us have lived with this toxic sludge trapped within our being since before we can remember, we think chronic low-grade unhappiness, anxiety, anger, guilt and shame are normal - *and for us, it IS normal!*

The occurrence of traumatic loss dumps its own heavy load of intense emotional energy onto the logjam of historical issues. This is like ingesting a heavy meal when we're already constipated. Now the system is *really* overloaded and strained. *Something has to give.* We either explode or implode.

The pain of grief is intensified when layers of repressed historical pain get stirred up and reactivated. At best, grief can serve as the purgative that eventually brings about in a thorough cleansing of repressed pain the mourner may have been carrying all their lives.

If you have ever been physically constipated, you know how uncomfortable that can be. You also know how much better you feel once the condition has been relieved and your lower intestines have been emptied! Similarly, when emotional constipation is relieved and your heart and soul have been emptied of historical and current pain, it's like getting a new lease on life!

For most people, expressing and releasing pain to reach grief resolution and integration is a process which takes place over a period of time. The time span may vary greatly from person to person depending on the nature of the loss and the context within which the person grieves. *There is no deadline.*

I would recommend that the pilgrim seeking grief resolution and integration maintain regular contact with their grief coach and companions for a minimum of a year to eighteen months. The intense pain of acute grief will lessen relatively quickly for most, but stay with the process.

Disregard those who tell you that you are overdoing it by continuing to meet with your grief companions. You're not. Most people do too little active, conscious grief work and they cheat themselves by doing so. Stay with it and reap the rewards.

One reward is that after you have been doing the work for a while you will be able to offer a calm, caring presence for others who grieve. This will be a priceless gift to the others but will also help to further resolve and integrate your own grief. We will discuss this more in a future chapter.

Amy Olshever, PhD, LCSW, is the Clinical Director of the COPE Foundation (www.copefoundation.org). In an article titled *"Breakdown or Catharsis? Crash or Cleanse?,"* she writes the following (with italics added for emphasis):

"Have you had the experience of making it through your day only to find that you are triggered by something totally unexpected, like a song on the radio? Or something that is usually inconsequential, like forgetting your shopping list, sets you off. Or sometimes, you have no idea what has set you off but there you are, crying, feeling overwhelmed and out of control.

"Often, when this happens people become angry and frustrated with themselves. *But this is a normal response to your grief.* In order to function throughout your day, each day, through the week, you have to maintain some measure of control. And often this involves *quieting, squashing or stuffing those feelings.* But after a while, it can build up and boil over. Hopefully, you can allow this to happen.

"If you are not in a place you can do this, try to get yourself there. Find someplace safe, quiet and *peaceful to allow this rush of emotion to wash up and out of you. Let yourself feel and release all of what you have been carrying around. And when it is done, for the moment, allow yourself to breathe. And know that you needed to release and relinquish what you were holding tightly inside.*

"This was a great message that you received from your physical and emotional self: *You need some self-care to work toward balancing having those feelings and letting them out so they don't take you by surprise so often.* Some options are to reach out to a friend, attend a support group, do some writing, seek out a therapist, get a massage, or take a Yoga class. What is your plan for self-care?"

Dr. Olshever describes eloquently what I call a "re-cycling event" and gives permission for expressing and releasing pain. I honor her credentials and her wisdom. I'm also grateful that I learned these things without the headache of getting a Ph.D.!

Like most things, expressing and releasing pain gets easier with practice and support. It becomes less and less scary as we learn from experience that feeling the pain will not kill us. If it would kill us, we would already be dead.

There is no reason for you to be afraid of feeling your feelings. The pain of feeling our feelings is temporary if we express and release the painful energy. If we hold onto it, the pain is eternal.

With grief comes an opportunity to develop life skills that will serve us in clearing away all kinds of historical pain along with the current pain of our grief. As we resolve and integrate our grief we become

- softer,
- stronger,
- wiser,
- more resilient,
- more empathetic,
- more compassionate, and
- more spiritually mature human beings.

I have compiled the following list of practices that will serve you in expressing and releasing your pain. Consider this a *menu of options* from which to choose, not necessarily a list of things to do. I have used all of these and can recommend them from personal experience. You can use any combination of options from this menu to your advantage.

- Breathe – Inhale and exhale and focus on the breath,

- Talk about the loss and your feelings in response to the loss,
- Write about the loss and your feelings in response to the loss,
- Draw, paint, sculpt, take photographs, try your hand at crafts (for example, creating a collage or scrapbook,) or use any other artistic medium to illustrate and express your grief,
- Pray and meditate (talk to and listen to your Higher Power) about the grief,
- Work up a sweat by any activity that stimulates deep breathing and produces perspiration,
- Get one or more professional therapeutic massages,
- Get one or more professional Reiki treatments,
- Scream into a pillow,
- Take a bowl full of ice cubes to a concrete or asphalt surface, hurl them one at a time onto the concrete and watch them shatter while breathing deeply and even yelling if you're in a private location,
- Cry,
- Listen to soulful music (music that makes you cry),
- Watch sad movies,
- Read literature that makes you cry,
- Get a plastic bat or an old tennis racket, breathe deeply, beat on pillows, and yell while doing this,
- Laugh,
- Anything else that connects you with your pain and brings it to your conscious awareness to be released.

While engaged in any of these practices, it is essential to maintain focused intention on *releasing* or *externalizing* your grief. Without focused intention to release, none of these practices will be especially helpful for grief resolution. With the focused intention of pouring out the pain in your heart, any of these practices individually or in any combination can be literally life-changing.

For example, talking about your loss can be extremely cathartic and cleansing *if you are consciously focused on releasing your pain as you talk*. If not, you can talk and talk and talk and little if anything is released and there is no resolution.

Without focused intention on releasing, crying may not be especially helpful. However, tears shed with positive intention can be cleansing and purifying.

In my most intense periods of grief work, I learned to feel and express anger without blaming anyone or anything. I learned that I could be angry about a situation and not blame myself or anyone else for the situation. Sometimes a situation just is what it is and *it's no one's fault*.

I heard once somewhere along the way that when we blame we give away our power. That made sense to me. We are empowered when we stop blaming ourselves or others and take full responsibility for our own actions and our own feelings.

I also learned to allow myself to experience and express sorrow and sadness without self-pity. What saves me from self-pity is a continual practice of gratitude. It's okay and even necessary to allow sadness and sorrow to surface and be expressed and released. On the same day I can count my blessings and avoid the toxic trap of self-pity.

Breathing slowly and deeply with focused attention to releasing pain can be extremely therapeutic in itself. Typically, when painful emotions come to our awareness, those of us conditioned by western culture will literally hold our breath until the pain is suppressed and goes back underground. We then become habituated to shallow breathing in an unconscious effort to avoid connecting with the pain.

Giving ourselves permission to breathe slowly and deeply can have significant benefits physically, emotionally, and spiritually. On those occasions when a re-cycling episode is suddenly triggered, just remembering to "breathe, breathe, breathe..." and blowing the pain out of our bodies with our breath can be very effective. One great thing that grief companions can do is to gently remind one another to breathe when intense feelings surface and are being expressed and released.

Writing about your loss and your emotional responses to the loss is extremely powerful. From the website of "What's Your Grief?" we find a great article titled "Five Benefits of Grief Journaling." I am including excerpts of it here, but I highly recommend the entire article found at https://tinyurl.com/y49xf3l4:

"Journaling is one of WYG's favorite, go-to, grief coping methods for many reasons. ... there are many psychological and physical benefits of grief journaling.

" ... We want to make sure you know _why_ this practice can be so beneficial and why it's worth your time and effort.

"REASON #1: Writing About Your Experiences Combats Avoidance...

"REASON #2: Physical Health Benefits of Journaling

"Research conducted by James W. Pennebaker and Joshua M. Smyth (available at https://tinyurl.com/y4tlrhqs) found that when people write about difficult and traumatic experiences, they sometimes reach a "letting go" state.

"When they researched the deeper physiological implications of this, they found ... When people went through a letting go experience while writing about their pain or trauma, their physical stress responses (things like heart rate and blood pressure) went way up. When they measured those things after people finished writing, their numbers dropped to lower than they had been to start and they stayed there.

"These findings have been replicated in follow-up physiological studies, including one where people who had heart attacks were split into two groups – one group who wrote their thoughts and feelings about the experience of having the heart attack and one group who wrote about neutral topics.

"The group who wrote about their feelings around the heart attack needed less prescribed medications, had fewer cardiac symptoms, and lower diastolic blood pressure than the group who didn't write about the experience and was still the case five months later. Crazy, right?

"Another study worked with individuals with asthma or rheumatoid arthritis who were split into two groups. One group was asked to write about the most traumatic experience of their life and the other to write about something neutral and benign. The results? The group who had asthma and wrote about a traumatic event had statistically significant improvements in lung function, those with arthritis had statistically significant improvements in joint health, whereas the control group didn't see these benefits.

"What is even more interesting is how dramatic the improvements were. People reported functional improvements that were on par with what would be expected when taking a new medication. Studies like this have now been repeated with those suffering from numerous other illnesses with similar results.

"REASON #3: Mental Health Benefits of Journaling
    "... Writing has been found to reduce symptoms of depression as well as anxiety.

"REASON #4: Better Sleep
    "For many reasons, grief can impact your sleep pattern. ... Research has found that writing or talking about worries, concerns, or other difficult thoughts before going to bed can reduce ruminative thoughts, help people fall asleep quicker, and improve the quality of sleep. ... better sleep equals improvements in overall functioning.

"REASON #5 WRITING is Beneficial for those Seeking Constructive Ways to Cope with Grief
    "... researchers conducted studies ...with individuals who had lost a loved one *and* who were looking for support in coping with their grief. The results of these studies showed that interventions like expressive writing were helpful for those who were grieving and looking for constructive ways to cope with their grief.

    "These studies and many others are outlined and referenced in the books by Pennebaker and Smyth available at https://tinyurl.com/y4tlrhqs

    "If you want help and motivation in establishing a grief-journaling practice, check out our e-course Self-Guided 30-Day

Grief Journaling Intensive available at https://whatsyourgrief.com/online-courses from which portions of this article were excerpted."

Note from Grace: When you go to the "What's Your Grief" website to look for this article, take some time to explore the entire range of excellent resources there. It is well worth your time.

Regarding Reiki sessions to assist with grief, I highly recommend the short article found at https://grief-reiki.com/how-can-reiki-help-with-grief/. There is additional excellent information available by doing an internet search using the words "reiki for grief and bereavement."

Regarding art therapy for grief resolution, consider "The therapeutic effectiveness of using visual art modalities with the bereaved: a systematic review," at https://tinyurl.com/y4lafcm4. Quoting from this article (with italics added),

"...this review critically evaluates the existent literature on the effectiveness of visual art modalities with the bereaved .... A total of 27 studies were included ... A narrative synthesis reports that *therapeutic application of visual art modalities was associated with positive changes such as continuing bonds with the deceased and meaning making* .... use of the visual arts has particularly burgeoned within the field in recent years. Visual arts such as drawing, painting, photography, and multimodal forms have been commonplace in grief therapy. ... *Participants (in the studies) overwhelmingly endorsed a positive subjective impact of the treatments incorporating visual art modalities. Across several studies, participants rated their well-being as significantly improved....*"

For more information on the use of expressive arts therapy for bereavement care, do your internet search using such search terms as "art therapy in grief support" or "expressive arts for the bereaved."

One of my favorite practices for inducing catharsis is listening to evocative music. Different genres of music work better for different people. When I needed assistance connecting with my grief, nothing worked better than listening to old-fashioned gospel hymns.

While on solitary road trips in the first few years after my mother's death, I would listen to cassette tapes of gospel hymns I knew from childhood. As I drove, I would weep and weep. It was wonderful. I still love those old hymns, even though they are not all congruent with my current theology ... but now I can listen to them without weeping.

By the way, I don't recommend weeping while driving. I'm grateful that my guardian angels protected me and other drivers while I released my grief. Now that I am older and wiser, I would not test my guardian angels in this way.

Regarding laughter as a practice for releasing grief, I like the quote by George Bernard Shaw who said, "Life does not cease to be funny when someone dies any more than it ceases to be serious when someone laughs." In my book titled *"Ten Simple Strategies for a Happier You: Changing the World from the Inside Out"* (available on amazon.com in both e-book and paperback formats), I have included an entire chapter on keeping and cultivating your sense of humor.

While one is grieving is a great time to practice lightening up with humor. You don't have to grieve all day and all night every day to make progress toward resolution and integration. You can give yourself a break with humor.

Experiment with these or other practices which bring your grief to the surface of your awareness to be expressed and released. Some of this can occur while you are alone but *for the full integration of your grief to be realized you must do at least some of this work in the presence of one or more others on the spiral pathway.* Any release work you do in solitude can be discussed with your companions.

In the next chapter we will consider a variety of sources from which you can receive healing positive energy to fill up the empty spaces created by catharsis.

For Personal Reflection, Journaling, and Group Discussion

1. In your own words, define catharsis.

2. "Spiritual beings on a human journey were *not* created to deny/hide/suppress feelings indefinitely, but were *always* intended to have, express and release emotional responses to life." Your response?

3. "At best, grief can serve as the purgative that eventually brings about in a thorough cleansing of repressed pain the mourner may have been carrying all their lives." Your thoughts?

4. Which practices recommended in this chapter do you think you will be most likely to use? Which will you be least likely to use?

CHAPTER 8

ACCEPT POSITIVE ENERGY

So we are inviting and allowing our grief to rise to the surface. We are creating time in our busy schedules to meet regularly with our grief coach and peer companions. When the feelings come up we do not push them back down. We don't self-medicate or zone out.

Instead, we breathe slowly and deeply, feel the feelings and release the emotional energy. As the grief comes into our conscious awareness we are getting it out, letting it out, and pouring it out. Great!

So now we give ourselves permission to take in:

- emotional support
- comfort
- kindness
- compassion
- sincere condolences
- concern
- caring
- love
- unconditional positive regard

...from the Universe to fill up the empty space that opened up in and around our hearts when the grief was released.

Yes, all of the words listed above are synonyms and can be located together in any *"Thesaurus."* I listed them here for your convenience and am purposely redundant for emphasis.

Every spiritual being on a human journey needs and deserves love. When we are grieving, we need and deserve extra love. It's okay to take in extra love during bereavement because there is plenty of love to go around. Accepting extra love at this time means you will have extra love to pass forward when you are ready to do so. We will discuss that more in the next chapter.

Open your heart and your mind to receiving love flowing to you through many channels. In addition to people, here is a list of sources of emotional support I have found to be meaningful and life-enhancing:

- Nature,
- Visual arts,
- Inspirational literature,
- Inspirational music,
- Inspirational television and movies,
- Spiritual practice,
- Animals.

You may already know of and/or discover others.

Yes, some of the love you need in order to reach grief resolution and grief integration can be received from sources other than humans *AND* at least some of the requisite positive energy must come from other humans on the spiral pathway.

...And yes, I know all about trust issues, betrayal, heartbreak, and disappointments when it comes to human relationships. I won't bore you with the details, but trust me. I have had my share of all of these. I survived intact thanks to countless angels who stood by me, loved me, and accepted me, warts and all.

So find your peeps, pour your heart out to them, and allow them to love you through the process. Soak up love from your peeps, from nature, from pets, from loving artists/poets/musicians/writers, and from Spirit. You cannot overdose on this medicine.

After you have been faithful to this practice for a span of time only you can determine, you may be ready to serve the human family by passing forward the kindness to others who are grieving. Please continue to the next chapter to consider this possibility.

For Personal Reflection, Journaling, and Group Discussion

1. "Every spiritual being on a human journey needs and deserves love. When we are grieving, we need and deserve extra love. It's okay to take in extra love during bereavement because there is plenty of love to go around." Your response?

CHAPTER 9

BECOME A GRIEF MENTOR

If you have been meeting regularly with a peer support group or with even one other pilgrim on the spiral pathway, you are already serving as a grief companion. If you are reading this in the early throes of intense grief and have not yet found your companions, don't be concerned at this time about becoming a mentor.

Take all the time you need to be the receiver of

- supportive attention,
- kindness,
- caring consideration,
- love,
- compassion, and
- sincere condolences.

For now, your job is to breathe and to feel, express and release your grief and to be a love sponge. Soak it up. There will be plenty of time later to pass it forward when you are ready.

However, please believe that if you persevere on the active, conscious grief journey you will eventually reach a plateau where you realize how far you have come. You will have acquired the ability to fully acknowledge the reality of the loss with your mind, heart, and soul. If your loss is that of a loved one who has died, perhaps with time you will have discovered ways to maintain meaningful bonds with that loved one, transcending the transition we call death.

You will have realized that your life will never be the same as it was before your loss. However, you will have also developed a willingness and a capacity to create a joyful life in the present while holding dear the memories of the past. You can also imagine a joyful future.

If you persevere on the spiral pathway, you will eventually realize that you have cultivated new skills and knowledge. You will have grown in wisdom and understanding. You will have the capability of enjoying serenity most of the time. As your times of conscious painful grieving eventually become less and less frequent and less and less severe, perhaps you will realize that grief and loss are simply a part of the experience of every spiritual being on a human pathway.

Perhaps you will eventually say, "Pain is not my enemy. Pain is my motivator and my teacher." At this point, we would say that you have become reconciled to the fact that pain, grief, and loss are all part of life for everyone on planet Earth along with an abundance of joy.

Looking back from this point, you will likely be eternally grateful to those who provided a caring presence for you when you were newly bereaved. They reassured you that you are not alone. They served as witnesses for your evolution.

When you stumbled, they helped you regain firm footing. When you fell, they picked you up. When you were bone tired, they encouraged you and gave you a hand. You know that without them you would never have come so far. As a tribute to those who were there for you when you needed them, you may have a desire to pass the kindness forward.

Consider this from Daisaku Ikeda, a Buddhist philosopher, educator, author, and nuclear disarmament advocate from Japan:

"There is no true joy in a life lived closed up in the little shell of the self. When you take one step to reach out to people, when you meet with others and share their thoughts and sufferings, infinite compassion and wisdom well up within your heart. Your life is transformed."

As you have released layer after layer of anger, sadness, guilt, shame, and fear, you have developed the ability to sit calmly with others who have experienced loss. You can now provide that priceless caring presence for others who are relative newcomers on the pathway. *This is not an obligation. It is a privilege.*

You know that you do not have to say "the right thing" to be an effective grief companion. You can sit quietly and patiently with others as they pour their hearts out. You know that all you really need to do while you sit with them is to breathe and listen ... slowly and deeply, inhale and exhale. If you say anything, it might be simply, "I hear you...and I care."

If you are involved in an on-going grief support group you may choose to continue attending group meetings to "hold the sacred space" energetically for others to do their grief work. If you are not a member of an on-going group, you may volunteer to serve in a bereavement ministry at your house of worship. You may volunteer at your local hospice.

You may make time to be a soul companion to anyone in your circle of influence who experiences traumatic loss of any kind. When you hear of a friend, family member, or acquaintance who is confronted with a difficult transition, you may go out of your way to express your caring and concern. You may go out of your way more than once for some people, depending on the situation.

You may send a card and/or take some "comfort food" to their home. You may take them a copy of this book if you have found it to be helpful. You may tell them about local resources you found to be helpful when you were new on the grief pathway.

You may invite them for coffee or tea and cookies. Over nourishment for the body you invite them to tell you how they are *REALLY* doing. You show them by your manner and your tone that it is *really okay* for them to tell you the emotional truth. Then you listen patiently without judging or giving advice.

When you practice this level of kindness for someone who is struggling with loss and grief, you are not only making a huge positive difference for this one person who is struggling but you are reinforcing your own grief resolution and integration. You are also raising the collective consciousness of the entire human family. *You are saving the world from the inside out.*

NOTE: If you doubt this to be true but are open to the idea and would like to read more about it, please read my previous book, *"Ten Simple Strategies for a Happier You – Changing the World From the Inside Out,"* at amazon.com.

At the time of this writing, the entire population of planet Earth is grieving the immeasurable losses of the global COVID-19 pandemic. There was a great unmet need for compassionate bereavement care BEFORE the pandemic. That need has only been multiplied infinitely by this worldwide health crisis and its economic repercussions.

At the same time the human family is struggling with the pandemic, we are also confronted with unprecedented political chaos, racial reckoning centuries in the making, and natural disasters created by the climate crisis. Pre-pandemic normalcy has been obliterated.

Just as individuals are changed forever by traumatic loss and grief, the entire ecosystem of planet Earth is changed forever by the collective losses resulting from the coronavirus and other events concurrent with this disease. The entire human family is grieving.

We each have individual lessons to learn from every challenge we encounter. On a much broader level we have lessons to learn collectively from this time in history if we are to evolve as a human family. Lest the suffering and sacrifice be in vain, we can each ask ourselves, *"What can I learn or re-learn from this? What is my lesson?"*

Maria Shriver is the niece of the assassinated President John F. Kennedy and the assassinated senator and presidential candidate Robert F. Kennedy. Her family experienced other traumatic losses. She is an excellent example of a woman who learned priceless lessons when she courageously faced her grief.

She wrote the following in the foreword to the Twentieth Anniversary edition of the book *"On Grief & Grieving,"* by David Kessler and Elisabeth Kubler-Ross, M.D. (Yes, this is the same Dr. Kubler-Ross we discussed in a much earlier chapter.) Maria's story illustrates and summarizes many of the ideas I have shared with you. She writes (italics added for emphasis):

"I grew up in a family that had lots of tragedy, but no one ever discussed it. I moved through those experiences, trying to make sense of the losses, without any guidance or framework for how to understand them.

"When I became an adult I realized that I was still trying to process what had happened, and I thought to myself that there must be a better way. ...*When my mother died... I experienced the true depth of grief... I had to face it; I had to really feel it.* It brought me to my knees. Then my uncle died two weeks after that. And then my father died a year and a half later. I was steeped in grief. ...

"*In my search for solace I found comfort in others who had gone through a death or multiple deaths. Every time I came across someone else's story of grief I felt a little less alone....*

"Grief can make a liar out of you. You say you are doing fine, when really your heart is shattered into a thousand tiny pieces. *But everyone wants you to say you're okay, so you do. We live in a culture that doesn't know how to grieve. We don't know how to experience pain, how to understand its process. We live in a society that wants us to get back to normal as soon as possible. We're expected to go back to work immediately, keep moving, to get on with our lives. But it doesn't work that way.*

"*We need time to move through the pain of loss. We need to step into it, really to get to know it, in order to learn how to live with it. In essence, that's what grief is. ... It's the moment when you stop trying to move on or change how much it hurts, and just let it out.*

"You think, What will I ever do? How will I survive...? But you do. *You survive. You don't go on the same, but you do go on. You learn that other people have gone through it. You find hope in their journeys. ...*

"*...grief has taught me that I can survive.* I used to be afraid that if I experienced grief it would overcome me and I wouldn't be able to survive the flood of it, that if I actually felt it I wouldn't be able to get back up. *It's taught me that I can feel it and it won't swallow me whole...*"

Maria found strength she didn't know she had. *This can be your story as well.*

One lesson I hope we collectively realize at a deeper level that ever before is this: *We are all connected.* Diverse sages, mystics, and scientists through the ages have agreed on this truth. One of them,

Dr. Martin Luther King, Jr., conveyed this sentiment eloquently when he said,

"It really boils down to this: that all life is interrelated. We are all caught in an inescapable network of mutuality, tied together into a single garment of destiny. Whatever affects one directly, affects all indirectly...We aren't going to have peace on Earth until we recognize the basic fact of the interrelated structure of all reality."

We will eventually emerge from the self-quarantine and the shadow of this plague, but the need for informed grief support will always and forever be part of the human drama. *Beloved reader, for your own sake please do your grief work. Also, do the work so that you can provide a caring presence for others who grieve. Please be part of the solution to the world's pain, first by attending to your own pain. Then, when you are ready, be a caregiver for others who grieve.*

For one more bit of inspiration and motivation, the following is a quote by award-winning author and social justice activist L.R. Knost (italics added):

"Do not be dismayed by the brokenness of the world.
All things break. All things can be mended.
Not with time, as they say, but *with intention.*
So go. Love intentionally, extravagantly, unconditionally.
The broken world waits in darkness
for the light that is you."

For Personal Reflection, Journaling, and Group Discussion

1. "Perhaps you will eventually say, 'Pain is not my enemy. Pain is my motivator and my teacher.'" Your response?
2. "There is no true joy in a life lived closed up in the little shell of the self. When you take one step to reach out to people, when you meet with others and share their thoughts and sufferings, infinite compassion and wisdom well up within your heart. Your life is transformed." (Daisaku Ikeda) Your thoughts?

3. "Maria (Shriver) found strength she didn't know she had. This can be your story as well." Your thoughts?
4. What is your reaction to the quote by L.R. Knost at the end of this chapter?

PART III
CONCLUDING THOUGHTS

CHAPTER 10

BRIEF MENTION OF COMPLICATED GRIEF

Dear reader, if you have given the suggestions in this book *your best good faith effort for at least a year* and have not yet experienced significant improvements in your state of mind and your overall quality of life, you may be suffering from what is called complicated grief. You can do an internet search on the words "complicated grief" and quickly gain some valuable information.

I recommend the material found on the Mayo Clinic website at https://tinyurl.com/vm4har7. If you go to this page which lists symptoms and causes, also go to the next page on the Mayo Clinic website on diagnosis and treatment of complicated grief at https://tinyurl.com/ydbsgeye.

If after doing your research on complicated grief you are concerned about your own well-being or the well-being of another, please do *not* try to definitively confirm or dispute a diagnosis even if you are a helping professional. Do not decide on your own if you or a loved one has or doesn't have complicated grief without seeking a second opinion. A degree of objectivity is necessary for accurate diagnosis.

Start by seeing your primary family practice doctor and tell the doctor in detail what you are experiencing. On the Mayo Clinic website at https://tinyurl.com/ydbsgeye there are excellent suggestions for preparing for a doctor's appointment to talk about your grief. There are also the kinds of questions you should expect from your doctor.

Your primary doctor may refer you to a specialist for assessment. If so, follow through and see the specialist as quickly as possible. If you are confident in the recommendations of the specialist, follow their instructions. If you do not feel confident in the recommendations of the first specialist, get a second opinion as soon as possible.

If you are diagnosed as having complicated grief and you are not already benefitting from working with a grief professional, it's important that you seek the services of a helping professional who has specialized training in facilitating grief resolution and integration. You can refer again to Chapter 6 and my suggestions for finding a professional who will be a good match for you.

If you are challenged with complicated grief, know that countless individuals have faced this challenge and not only survived but learned to thrive. Set an intention to find the help you need to get better. Then find it. An ancient Eastern proverb says, *"When the student is ready, the teacher appears."* Keep breathing, keep putting one foot in front of the other, and don't *ever* give up.

For Personal Reflection, Journaling, and Group Discussion

1. What is your overall reaction to this brief mention of complicated grief?
2. "An ancient Eastern proverb says, *'When the student is ready, the teacher appears.'*" Your reaction?

CHAPTER 11

"IT IS WELL WITH MY SOUL..."

In my experience, hope comes when we hear true stories of others who are overcomers. The following is a true story of a man with great sorrow and great faith. I offer it to you in closing to illustrate that faith in Something or Someone Greater than ourselves can be a great asset in resolving and integrating grief.

Horatio Spafford (1828-1888) was a prominent lawyer and real estate investor in Chicago. He and his wife, Anna, had one son and four daughters and lived a life of philanthropy and service through their church.

In 1871, their four-year-old son died of scarlet fever. A few months later the great Chicago fire wiped out the majority of their property holdings. In 1873, just two years later, tragedy struck again.

The Spaffords planned to visit Europe as a family, but Horatio was detained by an unexpected business matter. He sent Anna and the girls ahead with plans to join them as soon as the business matter could be settled.

On the voyage across the Atlantic, the ship carrying Anna and their four daughters struck another vessel and quickly sank. Of the five Spaffords, only Anna survived. She sent a telegram to Horatio bearing only the devastating words, "Saved alone."

We can only imagine Spafford's unutterable grief upon receiving the news. He sailed immediately to join and comfort Anna. On his own transatlantic voyage as his ship neared the place where his daughters had drowned, he wrote the lyrics for the hymn "It is Well with My Soul," now within the public domain.

> *"When peace like a river, attendeth my way,*
> *When sorrows like sea billows roll,*
> *Whatever my lot, thou hast taught me to say*
> *It is well, it is well, with my soul*
> *It is well*
> *With my soul*
> *It is well, it is well with my soul..."*

The hymn does not diminish or deny pain but rather proclaims that God is present in the midst of tragedies and is greater than tragedy. It focuses less on the enormous loss and more on where to find hope. No doubt Spafford's faith was tested by the death of his daughters, but his focus turned to the faithfulness of his Higher Power in the midst of his immeasurable grief.

Beloved reader, whatever your faith journey has been or hasn't been up until now, on the pathway of grief you may realize a greater awareness of your spirituality than you've ever known before. It's not within the scope of this book to explore this possibility thoroughly, but you can explore this possibility on your own if you choose.

I've already mentioned the chapter on spirituality in my previous book, *"Ten Simple Strategies for a Happier You..."* available on amazon.com. It clarifies the difference between spirituality and religion and offers a menu of options for exploring and nurturing your spirituality. I mention it again to remind you that I am available to you both through my earlier publication and through my website www.angelsabide.com.

There is an infinite wealth of excellent resources available to the spiritual seeker. Again I remind you, *"When the student is ready, the teacher appears."* Set your intention to find a spiritual practice that works for you now in your grief. You will find it. Then eventually you will also be able to say, "It is well with my soul."

I honor that Spirit within you which is holy, eternal, infinite, and divine.

For Personal Reflection, Journaling, and Group Discussion

1. "Beloved reader, whatever your faith journey has been or hasn't been up until now, on the pathway of grief you may realize a greater awareness of your spirituality than you've ever known before." Your response?

FINAL NOTE AND REQUEST

THANK YOU FOR READING MY BOOK!

Please go to www.facebook.com/Grace-Terrys-Angels and give me your honest feedback so that future editions of this book can improve. Then if my message has benefitted you and you honestly think others can benefit from it, please leave a review on Amazon.com. Your review will help others find me and know that my book is a worthwhile purchase.

Also, as I prepare for the publication and release of "The Spiral Pathway of Grief," I'm already planning a follow-up book which will most likely be titled something like, *"Readers Respond to The Spiral Pathway of Grief."* Please accept my invitation to contribute to the follow-up.

Send me an email with any part of your grief story that you would be willing to share with the world. Be sure to put the words "READER CONTRIBUTION" in the subject line of the email. You can contribute with full credit given to you or you can contribute anonymously if you prefer.

I'm interested in reading anything you would like to send me. Here are some writing prompts you can use to help get you started if you find this helpful.

1. What was the nature of your loss?

2. How did grief feel to you? Describe as best you can.
3. What did people around you say or do that was helpful? Not helpful?
4. What do you wish everyone everywhere knew about grief in general?
5. What do you wish everyone knew about *your* grief?
6. Which parts of this book were most meaningful and/or helpful to you?
7. Is there anything written here with which you disagree? Feel free to say so.
8. What have been the most helpful resources you have found to help you move forward on the grief pathway?
9. What are your plans for continuing to move forward?
10. How do you feel about becoming a grief companion, now or in the future?

You can respond to any one of these prompts, any combination of two or more, or none of them. If you send me an email and share any of your grief journey with me, I will respond.

Angels abide with you –
  Grace Terry
  grace@angelsabide.com
  www.angelsabide.com
  www.facebook.com/Grace-Terrys-Angels